D0934884

SILENCING THE SOUNDED SELF

NORTHEASTERN UNIVERSITY 1898–1998

Music advisor to Northeastern University Press   Gunther Schuller

SILENCING THE SOUNDED SELF

John Cage and the American Experimental Tradition

Christopher Shultis

Northeastern University Press   Boston

Northeastern University Press

Copyright 1998 by Christopher Shultis

Library of Congress Cataloging-in-Publication Data
Shultis, Christopher.
    Silencing the sounded self : John Cage and the American
experimental tradition / Christopher Shultis.
        p. cm.
    Includes bibliographical references and index.
    ISBN 1-55553-377-9 (cl : alk. paper)
    1. Cage, John—Criticism and interpretation. 2. Avant-garde
(Music)—United States. 3. Avant-garde (Aesthetics)—United States.
4. Thoreau, Henry David, 1817–1862—Influence. 5. Ives, Charles,
1874–1954—Influence. 6. Emerson, Ralph Waldo, 1803–1882—
Influence. 7. Music and literature. I. Title.
ML410.C24S58 1998
780'.973'0904—dc21   98-3642
                            MN

Designed by Ann Twombly

Composed in Trump by G & S Typesetters, Inc., Austin, Texas.
Printed and bound by Maple Press, York, Pennsylvania. The paper
is Sebago Antique, an acid-free sheet.

MANUFACTURED IN THE UNITED STATES OF AMERICA
02 01 00 99 98   5 4 3 2 1

FOR LESLIE AND MICHAEL

CONTENTS

ACKNOWLEDGMENTS

As I wrote and rewrote this book, many friends and colleagues offered their generous assistance. I thank first of all those who read and commented upon all or part of my work in manuscript or published form: Thomas Barrow, Lee Bartlett, Hanjo Berressem, Konrad Boehmer, Norman O. Brown, Thomas Dodson, Russell Goodman, Charles Hamm, Marjorie Perloff, Joan Retallack, Dieter Schulz, Richard K. Winslow, and two anonymous readers for Northeastern University Press. Special thanks go to Thomas DeLio and Gary Scharnhorst, who not only read and commented upon my work but also offered advice and expertise on numerous occasions.

I also had the privilege of sharing my ideas through lectures at the following institutions: Arizona State University West, Mills College, University of Maryland at College Park, Rheinisch-Westfälisch Technische Hochschule in Aachen, Ruprecht-Karls-Universität in Heidelberg, Heinrich-Heine-Universität in Düsseldorf, Maria Curie-Skłodowska University in Lublin, Poland, and Palacký University in Olomouc, Czech Republic.

My writing began during a sabbatical leave granted me by the Department of Music and the College of Fine Arts at the University of New Mexico. I also received research grants—two from the College of Fine Arts and one from the Research Allocations Committee at the University of New Mexico—that enabled me to visit the archives at the University of California at Santa Cruz, Northwestern University, and Wesleyan University that contain material related to John Cage. My contacts—Rita Bottoms at UC–Santa Cruz, Deborah Campana at Northwestern, and Elizabeth Swaim at Wesleyan—were, like the rest of the staff at these library collections, always courteous and helpful.

Finally, I acknowledge the constant support of my parents, Patricia and Terry Shultis, and thank my wife, Leslie, and my son, Michael, whose love and support richly deserve this book's dedication.

The last chapter of this book is a revised version of my essay "Silencing the Sounded Self: John Cage and the Intentionality of Nonintention," which appeared in *The Musical Quarterly*, vol. 79, no. 2 (Summer 1995): pp. 312–350. It is reprinted here by permission of Oxford University Press.

For permission to include material under copyright, grateful acknowledgment is made as follows:

Unless we go to extremes, we won't get anywhere.
—John Cage

We say one thing is not another thing.
Or sometimes we say it is.
Or we say "they are the same."
—Jasper Johns ("Sketchbook Notes")

Grey's differentiated. Johns.
—John Cage ("Diary")

[T]here is something which is, so to speak, nothing;
and moreover, a nothing which has nothing *in it.*
That's what the nothing in between *is.*
—John Cage (*For the Birds*)

Finally, with nothing in it to grasp, the work is
weather, . . . in oscillation with it we tend toward
our ultimate place: zero, gray disinterest.
—John Cage ("Jasper Johns")

INTRODUCTION

Context is a predominant concern in my study of John Cage. According to Jonathan Brent, "In Europe he is seen as characteristically American; in America he is seen as an anomaly."[1] This book will challenge the American perception of Cage as an outsider. The first three chapters place John Cage in a distinctively American historical context. Who are his predecessors and contemporaries and what resonates between their concerns and his? That context, determined by tracing Cage's intellectual interests, includes individuals such as Ralph Waldo Emerson, Henry David Thoreau, William Carlos Williams, Charles Olson, and Charles Ives, all longtime staples of Americanist scholarship. The results of such an investigation suggest that Europeans have a better sense of Cage's "American-ness" than do his fellow Americans.[2]

What follows is a study in extremes. It defines nothing. Rather, it places certain writers and composers into two camps, each of which is, in some sense, an extreme. All is not so black and white, of course. What interests me is the "nothing in between":[3] that interplay of black and white, two extremes that converge at zero and give rise to the richness of the color gray. By going to extremes, I mean to explore that richness and differentiate the grays.

My overall thesis is as follows: although the so-called American experimental tradition coheres through a common preference for process-oriented rather than goal-oriented artmaking, the issue of control is a specter in the midst of such apparent concord. A contextual study of how John Cage fits within the experimental tradition uncovers this distinction: does the artist control the process, or does the artist coexist as part of it? Reciprocally, this distinction builds a vocabulary for the comparative analysis of such issues in Cage's poetry and music.

Cage shied away from the matter of "influences," believing instead that one's own ideas attract historical precursors. In one of two statements on the composer Charles Ives, Cage observed: "We become, I believe, aware of the past by what we do."[4] Whether the past influences what we do or affirms what we do, one thing is certain. By following the trail of Cage's well-documented interests, one discovers an American tradition that provides a historical context for his creative work. Moreover, a study of Cage establishes the split of control versus coexistence within this tradition.

This book is not an attempt to pin down a body of artists under the rubric "experimental." Nor is it an attempt to define precisely what constitutes the "American experimental tradition."[5] It is governed by the assumption that an emphasis on process is a shared concern of all artists commonly regarded as "experimental."[6]

In general, experimental artists initiate processes because they are interested in results as "discoveries." They approach the making of art as an experiment that begins with a problem that is eventually resolved; hence their labeling as "experimental." The emphasis is on an open-ended approach, where the artist does not proceed with a set goal in mind.

Although processes can be constructed in a variety of ways, they are *initiated* in only two: by an artistic self that controls the process, or by an artistic self that coexists within that process. John Cage addressed this issue as follows: "Changed, mind includes even itself. Unchanged, nothing gets in or out."[7] The changed mind is an open mind, where the ego does not control the flow of experience. The unchanged mind is controlled by the ego, which stops the flow of experience. Thus, for Cage, an openly coexistent process required a "changed mind" that could allow outside and inside to coexist.

Although artistic control is a historically well documented phenomenon, tracing the development of artistic coexistence is not so easy. A study of the creative work of John Cage clarifies this distinction. A clue to the discovery of coexistence is what Cage has said was his most important legacy: "Having shown the practicality of making works of art non-intentionally."[8] Non-intention, as a desire to remove the self from the center of artistic discourse, points toward a tradition of artistic coexistence. And it is thanks to John Cage that we find its earliest American practitioner, Henry David Thoreau. As Cage has said, "Reading Thoreau's *Journal*, I discover any idea I've ever had worth its salt."[9] I will show non-intention to be one of those ideas.

Certain literary scholars see the writings of Thoreau as strikingly different from those of his erstwhile mentor, Ralph Waldo Emerson. For them, the younger man's work, his *Journal* in particular, departs from rather than continues the Emersonian tradition. John Cage shared this opinion. His passion for Thoreau was almost matched by his dislike for Emerson: "I found it very difficult to enjoy. I found it stuffy. . . . Emerson tends to get one idea and develop it." This development of ideas is a shaping of experience, an instance of artistic control. On the other hand, according to Cage, "Thoreau doesn't do that. There's an unexpectedness from sentence to sentence and paragraph to paragraph in Thoreau. One's constantly surprised and refreshed."[10] For Thoreau, observed experience need not serve merely as material to be shaped; instead, being interesting in and of itself, such experience need only be recorded.

In Emerson and Thoreau, one finds nineteenth-century precedence for issues of control and coexistence in artmaking. John Cage is a twentieth-century descendent of Thoreau's nonintentional approach. This invites the following question: does Emerson have a descendant in this century as well? The answer is found in the compositions and writings of Charles Ives. The "Emerson of American music,"[11] according to Betty E. Ch'maj, Ives carried the tradition of the controlling self into the twentieth century. Especially later in life, Ives was devoted to the writings of Emerson. As the "father of American music,"[12] and also regarded as the first representative of the experimental tradition in American music, Ives serves as an ideal contrast to John Cage. Ives's experimentalism is especially influenced by Emerson. Cage's experimentalism, as already noted, is preceded by Thoreau's. John Cage and Charles Ives represent the two poles of self (respectively, the coexisting and controlling) in American experimental music, connecting contemporary concerns to a nineteenth-century past.[13]

If Cage and Ives represent coexisting and controlling selves in music, is there a continuation of these ideas in twentieth-century American poetry? Would not poetry seem an even more likely candidate for a continuation of ideas that originate in the works of poets like Emerson and Thoreau? The answer to this question is also yes, and a study of John Cage greatly facilitates this investigation as well.

Emerson's importance to modern poetry is extensively documented.[14] However, this same scholarship pays far less attention to Thoreau. Not all experimental poets fit the description of Emerson's clearly defined poetic self. I intend to use the poles of control and coexistence to distinguish two important styles of experimental poetry: projective and objective verse. Placing Cage's writings in the context of twentieth-century American poetry allows Thoreau's aesthetic of coexistence to be seen as an alternative to the Emersonian self.[15]

The first three chapters of this book will place various experimental artists under the rubric of either control or coexistence. The first chapter compares Ives to Emerson (control); the next compares Cage to Thoreau (coexistence); and the third compares the controlling self found in projective verse (as written by Charles Olson, Robert Creeley, Edward Dorn, and Robert Duncan) with the coexistent self of the objectivists (including, among others, William Carlos Williams, Louis Zukofsky, George Oppen, and, of course, John Cage).

Placement will be determined by measuring these artists' poetics against three criteria. *First*, what is the artist's relation to nature? Is the creative self separate from nature (controlling), or is it an inseparable part of nature (coexisting)? A self in conflict with nature, or who sees nature as an "other" that must be subdued, is a controlling self. One who observes nature, an artist who looks on what is "outside" as something not separate from self, is a coexistent self. Further, the coexistent self is seen as part of something bigger than the individual self. Reality does not reside solely within one particular consciousness. Observing nature is a way of connecting known and unknown. The controlling self's desire, conversely, is to subdue, to make the unknown known and thus conquerable.

Second, what role does symbolism play in the artist's work? This study views symbols as abstractions that appropriate nature toward the transcendence of human meaning. In other words, symbols are a way of appropriating natural objects "as they are" and "developing" them into something that exists apart from their actual being. When symbols are used to effect such transcendence, the artists involved will be viewed as controlling selves. On the other hand, artists who do not emphasize the use of symbols in their work, who wish to observe nature in and of itself, will be regarded as coexisting selves. Many of the artists discussed will display both characteristic selves at some points. However, one or the other approach always tends to predominate, and that determines placement.

Third, and finally, is the artist's work closed or open to the unintentional? In some cases, the answer will be determined by considering the artist's approach to nature and symbolism. The latter is a decidedly closed form of representation. If a dominating relation to nature helps determine the artist's aesthetic view, symbolism is frequently a manifestation of that aesthetic in the making of art. This will be particularly evident in the first chapter. In other cases, intention versus non-intention is an outright concern. A prominent example of such in this book is the connection between sound and silence in music and between projection and observation in poetry. In both instances, one approach (sound, projection) views the self or creation as separately *in* the environment, whereas the other approach (silence, observation) views the self as an inseparable part *of* the environment.

By the end of the third chapter, clear distinctions will have been drawn illustrating the difference between control and coexistence in the creative self. The first will involve a controlling or coexistent connection with nature; the second, symbolism versus the thing itself; and the third, intention versus non-intention, manifested as either projection/observation or sound/silence. The obvious conclusion is that these aesthetic distinctions posit either dualism or nondualism in one form or another.

In the last chapter, I will show how nondualism manifests itself, in both text and music, through Cage's attempt to "silence the self." For Cage, sound and silence, something and nothing are unopposed; they coexist. He frequently used the *Ten Ox Herding Pictures* (which illustrate, according to the beliefs of Zen Buddhism, the road to enlightenment) as an example of such coexistence.[16] In the tenth picture, after experiencing emptiness, the Ox Herder returns home bearing gifts. Therefore, something and nothing are seen as coexistent. In the epigraphs opening this introduction, Cage speaks of a something that has nothing in it. And, for him, something and nothing coexist only through the silent practice of non-intention.

Cage was not only a composer; he was also a writer and visual artist. These genre distinctions are very real in his work. However, it is difficult to separate one from the other when attempting to write a critical study. It is problematic at best to establish a hierarchy that regards Cage as composer first, philosopher second, and so on. As an illustration of such difficulties, one might refer to Cage's interest in a particular haiku by Basho:

pine mushroom
ignorance   leaf of tree
adhesiveness

Ultimately, Cage's version of this poem became:

What mushroom?
What leaf? [17]

James Pritchett has observed that "[t]o ignore the music and then attempt to write about the philosophy is putting the cart before the horse."[18] Should we infer, then, that music is the appropriate horse? Cage himself has said that "they ask me sometimes which I think are more important—my compositions or music or my texts, and the answers are the ones we've been giving all through this conversation—when we're writing music, that's what's important, and when we're writing ideas, that's what's interesting."[19]

To place any of Cage's work, whether music, text, or philosophy, as either cart or horse is to miss the marvelously coexistent nature of his art. One might respond to the construction of such hierarchies with lines similar to the final version Cage made of Basho's:

What cart?
What horse?

Cage's music and ideas need not be separated in the act of criticism. And that goes for his texts as well. Cage's ideas have both fueled and been fueled by his creative activity. Cage wrote texts for nearly as long as he wrote music. One does not lead to another. Instead, they run parallel with each other.

To allude once more to Basho, my study emphasizes the issue of "adhesiveness." Thus, in the final chapter I look at several of Cage's works in which music and text in a certain sense adhere and "become" one another. Cage suggests as much in his first published collection, *Silence:* "as I am engaged in a variety of activities, I attempt to introduce into each one of them aspects conventionally limited to one or more of the others."[20]

In the last chapter, issues consistent with the first three chapters are directly considered in Cage's writings and scores. Textual analysis will show a movement from "something" (the introduction of his musical forms into syntactically determined texts) to "nothing" (where texts lose semantic meaning and become sounds in and of themselves). In other words, I will trace how Cage's writings move from intention to non-intention, just as his music did when he wrote *4'33"*, the so-called silent piece, in 1952. In that work, the pianist merely sits at the piano, the only sounds being the unintended ones found in the performance environment. As something becomes nothing, intention moves to non-intention, and text as sound becomes music.

Cage has said that he wished to "musicate" language. This sentiment can be traced to several of his earliest lectures.[21] The initial attempt is to somehow "formalize" writing in a way that for Cage produces poetry: "As I see it, poetry is not prose simply because poetry is in one way or another formalized. It is not poetry by reason of its content or ambiguity but by reason of its allowing musical elements (time, sound) to be introduced into the world of words."[22] One may differ with Cage's definition of poetry. However, it is an excellent description of his development as a writer of texts.

At first these writings include what may be regarded as "musical time." Although phrases and sentences retain conventional syntax, they are structured according to time lengths that do not always mirror the inflections of speech. According to Cage, "It has been my habit for some years to write texts in a way analogous to the way I write music."[23] He does so by applying structural methods to the writing of text previously designed for his music compositions.

Ultimately, Cage begins to introduce concepts of "music as sound" into his writings. His interest was in freeing language from conventional structures and meanings. This is fully accomplished in "Empty Words," a lecture in four parts, each lasting two and a half hours with a half hour break between. "Empty Words" continues the task begun with "Mureau."[24] This work subjected to chance operations all references to music and sounds appearing in the *Journal* of Henry David Thoreau. These might be sentences, phrases, words, syllables, or letters. In "Empty Words," Cage removes the sentences and initiates a direction where phrases, words, syllables, or letters are dropped one by one in each succeeding lecture until the final text consists of nothing but letters and empty space. Without semantic reference, language becomes sounds in the way music is sounds. Text and music coexist as one.

Contexts are fluid, not fixed. Placing Cage within experimental traditions of poetry and music shows how such work fits within these separate disciplines. However, this book concludes by emphasizing movement: from music to text, text to music. Cage himself serves as a door between the "rooms" of poetry and music. Following the distinction of coexisting and controlling selves that forms the heart of my analysis, Cage's "door" is transparent: a "nothing between" constituting that gray area where the black and white of distinctively different genres meet.

PART ONE/MUSIC

*I have never believed that any one individual could
speak for an entire continent, in all its variety of cultures
and societies. Nor has it ever seemed reasonable to me to
believe that there could ever be one single "mainstream
of music." . . . In any case it seemed to me even then that
to be American was to honor difference, and to welcome
the experimental, the fresh and the new, instead of trying
to establish in advance the road our creative life should
follow.*

—Henry Cowell (*American Composers on American Music*)

Part One will consider the distinction of self in twentieth-
century American experimental music by locating that distinction with nineteenth-century predecessors. It will examine the
aesthetic writings of the composers Charles Ives and John Cage
and those of their respective mentors, Ralph Waldo Emerson and
Henry David Thoreau.[1] Concerning Charles Ives, Howard Boatwright has written: "If music itself were his concern, he wrote
music. But he used words to provide the general philosophical

support for his compositions."[2] The analysis that follows shares Ives's point of view, addressing aesthetic issues that inform the making of experimental music rather than specifically discussing music as it is actually heard.

The very notion of an "experimental tradition" may, at first, seem oxymoronic. How can experiment, whose fundamental concern is the discovery of the unknown, intersect with tradition, a word that, by nature, is concerned with history and with what is already known? The answer is simply this: experiment has a history in America.[3] What Hyatt H. Waggoner has written about poetry may be extended to experimental American art-making as a whole: "From the beginning, the most representative American poets have anticipated the characteristic that more than anything else distinguishes the American poetry of our own day from that of the past and of other societies: in it *nothing* is known, nothing given, everything is discovered or created, or else remains in doubt."[4] Without specifically claiming experiment as its source, Waggoner describes a context out of which writers make what he considers to be characteristically American poetry. However, his description could easily serve as a definition of experiment. And it is that American characteristic which is both the source and, more critically, the method that underlies such artistic making.

Interest in experiment is a connecting theme for Emerson and Thoreau, Ives and Cage. However, experiment, by definition, has two forms. The first, "an act or operation carried out under conditions determined by the experimenter in order to discover some unknown principle or effect," posits an open-ended project with no specific results anticipated. However, the second definition, "to test, establish, or illustrate some suggested or known truth," demonstrates a clearly preconceived intention on the part of the experimenter. The first definition holds no expectations, since what will be discovered is unknown. The second, however, does bring expectations into the experiment, making it quite different from the first definition.

Thus, the two poles of experiment are the "unknown" versus the "truth." It is especially important to note that truth is "suggested or known" and that the experiment is *intended* to "test, establish or illustrate" it. In establishing the known, the experimenter brings a very specific intent to the experiment, that of illustrating "some suggested or known truth." Such intentions are shared by both Emerson and Ives: the experiment is never complete until conclusions have been drawn and the "truth" in it has been found. In seeking the unknown, on the other hand, the experimenter simply establishes the "conditions," or method, behind the experiment without preconceptions about the results. This is the experimentalism I find in the work of Thoreau and Cage: following a method of observation without intentionally drawing conclusions.

Cage and Ives are central figures in the experimental tradition for many reasons, of which three are pertinent here. First, Ives wrote all his works well before World War II (most before World War I), whereas most of Cage's influential ideas (at least for this study) appear after World War II. Thus, Cage may be regarded as a second-generation successor to Ives's musical experimentalism. The year 1945 is often viewed as a stylistic benchmark in music history. Cage and Ives divide the century in similar fashion, and their differences may well be attributable to their historical placement.

Second, I find that the experimental tradition's literary precursors are nineteenth-century writers of the Concord school, Emerson and Thoreau in particular.[5] Of those composers regarded as part of the experimental tradition, only Cage and Ives specifically refer to the transcendentalists of Concord. In addition, Ives and Cage align themselves with Emerson and Thoreau respectively, thus mirroring the first- and second-generation distinctions of their nineteenth-century predecessors.

Ives was profoundly influenced by the writings of the transcendentalists, particularly Emerson and Thoreau. He is regarded as the first composer to put the ideas of transcendentalism within the context of musical composition.[6] Even though Ives claimed an affinity with both Emerson and Thoreau, it is

Emerson who is regarded as the primary influence on his aesthetic views.[7] Cage did not share Ives's appreciation of Emerson; he did, however, greatly admire the work of Henry David Thoreau.

This disparity is reflected in the literary scholarship available to the two composers. In the early decades of this century, Emerson was regarded as the dominant figure of the Transcendental school. Thoreau was considered a lesser, complementary figure who essentially parroted the aesthetic positions of his mentor.[8] This was the prevailing view when Ives formulated his mature aesthetic. However, in the 1940s Thoreau scholarship began to diverge from this opinion.[9] In the 1960s, when John Cage discovered Thoreau, such distinctions were being fully addressed.[10] There is now a strong consensus that Thoreau is no longer a "lesser figure." And although he is still seen by many as continuing certain Emersonian ideas, a growing body of scholarship shares Cage's opinion that Thoreau's writings, especially his *Journal*, differ fundamentally from some of Emerson's aesthetic views.[11]

Third, and finally, Cage and Ives embody the distinction I find between coexistent and controlling artistic selves. As such, they carry the nineteenth-century differences of their respective predecessors, Thoreau and Emerson, into the twentieth century.

In what follows, I will address a common interest in experimentalism while delineating two strikingly different experimental approaches. My analysis will consider affinities between Cage and Thoreau, Emerson and Ives. This part of the book concerns the issue of intention, with a particular emphasis on the question of dualism versus nondualism. Cage and Thoreau share a nondualistic interest in sound and silence; although usually regarded as opposites, they are for Cage and Thoreau part and parcel of the same thing. Emerson and Ives strive toward monistic unity, a reconciliation of opposites. Such an effort requires an initial dualism that is unified by a purposeful intent. Two such dualisms are readily found in their work: for Emerson, a dual relationship between humanity and nature; for Ives, his famous compositional duality between "substance" and "manner."[12]

In the context of this book, dualism expresses itself through human control and a desire for unity that employs what is known as transcendental correspondence, a form of symbolism central to the aesthetics of Emerson and Ives. Nondualism, as found in the creative work of Thoreau and Cage, shifts away from a controlling self toward multiplicity and the acceptance of things as they are, thus rejecting the idea of correspondences between human symbols and natural things.

DUALISM/UNITY/CONTROL
Ralph Waldo Emerson and Charles Ives

Heard melodies are sweet, but those unheard
  Are sweeter; therefore, ye soft pipes, play on;
Not to the sensual ear, but, more endear'd,
  Pipe to the spirit ditties of no tone.
—John Keats ("Ode on a Grecian Urn")

I will now address certain affinities between Ralph Waldo Emerson and Charles Ives. After briefly describing their experimentalism, I will show that they hold similar aesthetic views regarding the inherently dual relation between humanity and nature. Both identify art as capable of unifying the two via the use of a particular symbolic practice called transcendental correspondence.

The first necessary question may initially seem obvious: does Emerson belong in the experimental tradition? At odds with such an association is his well-known allegiance to idealism. As Russell Goodman has written, "Because he is an 'idealist,' it might seem that Emerson must be committed to the idea, which attracted Hegel and Plato, of a completed and unchanging account of the world."[1] In his essay "History," Emerson seems to support such a view: "always the thought is prior to the fact; all the facts of history pre-exist in the mind as laws."[2] Mentioning thought as "prior to the fact" clearly suggests idealism. Further, his consideration of historical facts as pre-existent laws of the mind implies a fixed rather than open-ended worldview. However, Goodman goes on to say that "Emerson is committed to experimentation; his idealism is, as Dewey's was to be, experimental."[3] Emerson describes his experimentalism in the essay "Circles": "[L]et me remind the reader that I am only an experimenter. Do not set the least value on what I do, or the least discredit on what I do not, as if I pretended to settle any thing as true or false. I unsettle all things. No facts are to me sacred; none are profane; I simply experiment, an endless seeker with no Past at my back."[4] Emerson seems to proclaim two differing views when one compares the quotation from "Circles" to his words in "History." In the former, Emerson describes an experimental process similar to that of my first definition of experiment: an open-ended process with no fixed results. In the latter, Emerson speaks of "laws" existing "prior to facts" that are located in the mind, a fixed conception of the universe that seems to contradict his earlier notion of experimentalism. How can one reconcile such difference?

Idealism, as practiced by Emerson, consists of fixed laws that exist *a priori* to our experience. These laws, however, must be reconciled to experience and the results then disseminated by the experimenter. Emerson himself finds such reconciliation in the "soul." In the sentence immediately following the words just cited from "Circles," Emerson continues: "Yet this incessant movement and progression which all things partake could never become sensible to us but by contrast to some principle of fixture or stability in the soul" (SE, p. 236). And, from its very beginning, "Circles" still puts humanity in the center: "the eye is the *first circle*; the horizon which *it* forms is the second" (SE, p. 225; emphasis added).

One place where the soul is located is *within* humankind. In "The Over-Soul" Emerson remarks: "[W]ithin man is the soul of the whole; the wise silence; the universal beauty, to which every part and particle is equally related; the eternal ONE. And this deep power in which we exist and whose beatitude is all accessible to us, is not only self-sufficing and perfect in every hour, but the act of seeing and the thing seen, the seer and the spectacle, the subject and the object are one" (EE, p. 190). Such unity is an important aspect of Emerson's aesthetics; note, too, that it requires an "act of seeing," in other words a human act, to make subject and object "one."

Emerson's dualisms center on the separation of humanity and nature. They can be found throughout his writings. For Emerson, "subject and object are one" within the "soul." Whereas humanity partakes of the soul, nature does not. As he puts it in *Nature:* "Philosophically considered, the universe is composed of Nature and the Soul. Strictly speaking, therefore, all that is separate from us, all which Philosophy distinguishes as the NOT ME, that is, both nature and art, all other men and my own body, must be ranked under this name, NATURE" (SE, "Introduction," from *Nature,* p. 36). This is a dualistic view.

Examining the chapter "Idealism" (from *Nature*) clarifies this issue. Emerson describes nature's laws as permanent: "Any distrust of the permanence of laws would paralyze the faculties of man. Their permanence is sacredly respected, and his faith therein is perfect. The wheels and springs of man are all set to the hypothesis of the permanence of nature" (SE, p. 63). But its actual existence may not be: "[W]hilst we acquiesce entirely in the permanence of natural laws, the question of the absolute existence of nature still remains open. It is the uniform effect of culture on the human mind, not to shake our faith in the stability of particular phenomena, as of heat, water, azote; but to lead us to regard nature as phenomenon, not a substance; to attribute necessary existence to spirit; to esteem nature as an accident and an effect" (*SE*, p. 63.) According to Emerson, spirit is permanent, as natural laws are permanent. The existence of nature as a "substance," on the other hand, is in doubt.

If nature's existence is uncertain and "spirit" is fixed, where is spirit located? In nature or somewhere else? The answer comes when Emerson compares "Reason" with the senses, and then discusses the "effects of culture." For Emerson, a belief both in the absolute existence of nature and in an inherent unity between humanity and nature originates in "the senses and the unrenewed understanding": "In their view man and nature are indissolubly joined" (*SE*, p. 63). However, Emerson goes on to say: "The presence of Reason mars this faith. The first effort of thought tends to relax this despotism of the senses which binds us to nature as if we were a part of it, and shows us nature aloof, and, as it were, afloat" (*SE*, p. 63). "Reason" prevails over the mere "faith" of our senses, moving away from an erroneous belief in nondualism toward the accurate knowledge of dualism.[5]

In "Intellect," Emerson writes of hierarchies of nature: "Water dissolves wood and iron and salt; air dissolves water; electric fire dissolves air." He then places the intellect, which he locates in the mind, above all: "but the intellect dissolves fire, gravity, laws, method, and the subtlest unnamed relations of nature in its resistless menstruum" (*EE*, p. 229). And what is the goal of such power over nature? "Its vision is not like the vision of the eye, but is union with the things known" (*EE*, p. 229). Such union, however, occurs apart from nature, apart even from the self that originates it: "Intellect separates the fact considered, from *you*, from all local and personal reference, and discerns it as if it existed for its own sake" (*EE*, pp. 229–230). This seems to imply a position similar to Kant's thing-in-itself. Unlike Kant, however, Emerson takes the fact's existence apart from its sensual experience and places it in the realm of the ideal.[6]

What follows is critical to this analysis. For Emerson, comprehending a dualistic relation between humanity and nature leads to emancipation: "Nature is made to conspire with spirit to emancipate us. Certain mechanical changes, a small alteration in our local position, apprizes us of a dualism" (*SE*, "Idealism," from *Nature*, p. 64). These mechanical changes include ships, balloons, coaches, trains, camera obscuras. What these produce is an altered perception of things that "gives the whole world a pictorial air" (*SE*, "Idealism," from *Nature*, p. 64). Does Emerson consider this a reason why our senses cannot be trusted? No. Instead he sees it as confirming the separation between humanity and nature: "In these cases, by mechanical means, is suggested the difference between the observer and the spectacle—between man and nature. . . . [W]hilst the world is a spectacle, something in himself is stable" (*SE*, "Idealism," from *Nature*, p. 65). Thus, although the world is not fixed, humanity is. And even though Emerson sees spirit present "throughout nature," spirit "does not build up nature around us, but puts it forth through us, as the life of the tree puts forth new branches and leaves through the pores of the old" (*SE*, "Spirit," from *Nature*, p. 73). Humanity is the stable force, nature's source for the influx of spirit, and the harmony between nature and humanity is effected by "spirit" through the human self. Elsewhere in *Nature* (his first book) Emerson comments: "The greatest delight which the fields and woods minister is the suggestion of an occult relation between man and the vegetable. I am not alone and unacknowledged. They nod to me, and I to them." This might, at first, seem to suggest that he did not regard humanity and nature as separate. However, in the following paragraph, Emerson completes his thoughts: "Yet it is certain that the power to produce this delight does not reside in nature, but in man, or in a harmony of both" (*SE*, "Nature," from *Nature*, p. 39). This sentence, which seems uncertain at best, actually clarifies Emerson's position. The "delight" he speaks of is a relationship between humanity and nature. Initially it does not reside in nature, "but in man." However, he then professes the possibility of "a harmony of both." I find such initial separation followed by a possible harmony to be an early example of Emerson's belief that if unity is possible it requires a human act. Thus, it is the human self that establishes a hierarchy in which humanity is placed in a controlling position above nature.

For Emerson, the human self is in control. The universe is dualistic and harmony is achieved, if at all, only through human means. Translated aesthetically, Emerson sees the poet's role as attaining this initial recognition of dualism and then attempting to achieve harmony: "He unfixes the land and the sea, makes them revolve around the axis of his primary thought, and disposes them anew. . . . The sensual man conforms thoughts to things; the poet conforms things to his thoughts. The one esteems nature as rooted and fast; the other, as fluid, and impresses his being thereon" (*SE*, "Idealism," from *Nature*, p. 65). Humanity and nature are thus initially dual. The artist, by "conforming things to his thoughts," establishes harmony between them by "impressing his being thereon." As I will point out, this is exactly opposite to what Thoreau and Cage regard as the role of the artist-poet.

IVES

Aesthetically, Charles Ives is best considered a bridge between the two kinds of experimentalism this book describes.[7] He appreciates both Emerson and Thoreau; John Cage, on the other hand, appreciates Thoreau but has a distaste for Emerson.[8] The nature of the older composer's views also explains why John Cage admired only certain aspects of the music of Ives.[9]

The musical experimentalism of Charles Ives is well documented.[10] According to David Nicholls, "Ives's experimentalism is of two basic kinds: 1. the production of overtly experimental works in which, generally speaking, he tries out new compositional techniques; 2. the production of music in an unprecedentedly wide variety of supposedly exclusive musical styles and, more importantly, the integration of these styles into a pluralistic whole."[11] It is the second kind of experimentalism that concerns me here, since integration into a "pluralistic whole" is closely related to Emerson's goal of unity. In fact, they have so much in common that Betty E. Ch'maj can note, "Ives identified with Emerson so completely that it is often difficult to tell in his writings where one leaves off and the other begins." [12] And according to Rosalie Sandra Perry, "Many of Ives' ideas paralleled Emerson's, and Ives may even have patterned his own life-style after the great philosopher." [13]

With regard to Emerson, I have addressed three areas: dualism, idealism, and self. These ideas are also fundamental for Ives. As J. Peter Burkholder puts it, "There are three major foundations for Ives's thought in the *Essays* and most of his other writings from the 1910s and 1920s: (1) a dualistic approach to issues, (2) a personal and social idealism, and (3) a reliance on personal intuition and experience rather than external authority." [14]

Dualisms permeate Ives's thoughts in both musical and extramusical situations. His longest single essay, "The Majority," poses "the Majority—the People" versus "the Minority—the Non-People." Burkholder cites several other dualities. [15] The most famous is that of "substance and manner," which Ives regarded as "a fundamental duality in music, and in all art for that matter." [16] According to Burkholder, substance and manner is "the most critical duality for Ives's aesthetic." [17] The composer termed "substance" as an instance of "moral strength," which "suggests the body of a conviction which has its birth in the spiritual consciousness, whose youth is nourished in the moral consciousness, and whose maturity as a result of all this growth is then represented in a mental image" (*EB*, "Epilogue," p. 75). "Manner," on the other hand, is simply the means by which substance is "translated into expression" (*EB*, "Epilogue," p. 75). In the "Epilogue" of his *Essays* (where this distinction is addressed), Ives determines the compositional greatness of several composers by deciding whether their work stems from substance or manner. "Substance" is born of the "spirit," which Emerson regarded as separate from nature, and it is "nourished in the moral consciousness," which Ives regarded as dualistic. [18] For Ives, "substance can be expressed in music, and that . . . is the only valuable thing in it" (*EB*, "Epilogue," p. 77). Thus, substance in music, as a solely human practice, is grounded in separation, polarity, and dualism.

For Ives, as with his mentor Emerson, it was a human responsibility to attempt to unify not only humanity and nature but all experience, including "real" and "transcendental." According to Wilfred Mellers, "While Ives did not believe that the Real and the Transcendental . . . could be reconciled in the conditions of temporal mortality, he believed that it was the duty of every man to attempt such reconciliation."[19] That Ives thus subscribed to such distinctions of "real" and "transcendental" is further evidence of his idealism. Like Emerson, he believed in an absolute that existed outside the reality of nature: a "universal mind" that is essentially "spirit" and contains within itself "the permanence of natural laws." Emerson expresses his vision of it as "that Unity, that Over soul, within which every man's particular being is contained and made one with all other" (*EE*, "The Over-Soul," p. 189). Ives himself writes as much; in fact, he might have had this passage in mind when he remarked: "To Emerson, unity and the over-soul, or the common-heart, are synonymous. Unity is at least nearer to these than to solid geometry, though geometry may be all unity" (*EB*, "Epilogue," p. 99). Ives saw unity as residing within the "over-soul," outside the unified geometry of nature. In this regard, compare Emerson's remark that "within man is the soul of the whole; the wise silence; the universal beauty, to which every part and particle is equally related; the eternal ONE" (*EE*, "The Over-Soul," p. 190). It is important to emphasize that when Ives writes "for the truth of substance is sometimes silence" (*EB*, "Epilogue," p. 90) it is the "wise silence" of Emerson, a silence that comes from within the self. As I will demonstrate, this silence is a far cry from the unintentional silence of Cage and Thoreau.

Ives's *Concord Sonata* (*Second Pianoforte Sonata, "Concord, Mass., 1840–1860"*) uses the opening motif from Beethoven's *Fifth Symphony* as a unifying device throughout. For Ives, it represented the desire to "strive to bring it [the motif] towards the spiritual message of Emerson's revelations . . . the soul of humanity knocking at the door of the divine mysteries, radiant in the faith that it *will* be opened—and the human become the divine!" (*EB*, "Emerson," p. 36). Ives considered Beethoven "the best product that human beings can boast of" (*EB*, "Epilogue," p. 88),[20] and according to Wilfred Mellers: "Like Beethoven, whom he revered above all creators, he [Ives] saw the sonata as an attempt to impose the unity of the Will on the chaos of experience; and his awareness of contradiction (like Beethoven's) was so violent that it had ultimately to seek resolution in a transcendental act."[21]

What constitutes the "transcendental act" shared by Beethoven and Ives that enabled them to "impose the unity of the Will" in their compositions? Harmony. In Henry Cowell's view, "Ives has always had a strong interest in harmony."[22] The usual musical definition of harmony suggests the existence of vertical relationships between pitches. This is obviously what Cowell has in mind when he notes that there are "always relationships to be found; they are usually built on a rather complex harmonic concept."[23] Cowell goes on to say that "even when Ives's voices seem most independent, the melodies are bound together by a strong harmonic feeling."[24]

This book is concerned, however, with the aesthetics behind the music rather than the music itself. In this context, it is the idea of unity translated into musical harmony that is paramount. This is the reason behind Ives's interest in the sonata as a form: "[H]e finds one principle of unity in the sonata, because it deals with the resolution of two contrasting themes. The two-sidedness of reality, all the paradoxes of existence, are present to all Ives's thinking."[25] Thus does Henry Cowell describe Ives's desire to unify the dualisms of experience through music. Moreover, as an expression of Ives's idealism, such unification was an attempt to reconcile real and ideal: "he believes that full expression of the opposing aspects of any idea whatever is a necessary step on the way to perfect truth, since only in this way can the common basis for the integration of these opposites be found."[26] Finally, Ives sees such activity as a distinctly human struggle, where truth can only be approached by human control:

> Ives's interest is in this *process toward* integration; . . . he envisages a series of integrations of dualities, each of which as it is achieved is seen as a sort of partial or temporary truth, a truth which then becomes only one aspect of another set of opposites which sooner or later must be resolved in its turn. This struggle toward truth and integration is the nearest man can come to absolute truth, in Ives's view; but he feels the very effort required imparts a certain unity and coherence of its own.[27]

Ives and Emerson each had a close relationship with nature. However, nature is but a means for human expression. For example, Ives (speaking with the "voice" of Emerson) remarks: "I'm thinking of the sun's glory today and I'll let his light shine through me. I'll say any damn thing that this inspires me with" (*EB*, "Emerson," p. 23). There is no question that he intends to speak of nature, that it is nature's inspiration of which he will speak. However, the point of origin for the speech is Ives himself. His stance calls to mind what Ralph Waldo Emerson wrote in *Nature:* "I become a transparent eyeball; I am nothing; I see all; the currents of the Universal Being circulate through me; I am part or parcel of God" (*SE*, "Nature," p. 39). The inspiration may come from without, but its expression is formed from within. The human self is both central to and in control of such expression.

As I have demonstrated, Emerson and Ives subscribe to the tenets of idealism and experimentalism. They also wish to unify experience. In Emerson's case, unity is found through idealism, where ideas of the mind (both individual and universal) are reflected in the world of nature. However, the thread that connects the world of nature to the world of ideas lies not in nature but in the human mind. Ives embodied Emerson's views aesthetically by attempting to impose unity in his artistic creations. Betty E. Ch'maj declares that Ives's "constant aim was to try to impose unity upon the multiple layers of experience."[28] In both cases, such unity is only possible through human action. For Emerson and for Ives, dualism is our natural state; only through human control can unity be attained.

SYMBOLISM

In the work of both Emerson and Ives, human control finds its way into art through symbolic abstraction. For Emerson, experiments are not open-ended at all but depend upon the fixity of law, inherently a part of human consciousness: "[W]e bring with us to every experiment the innate universal laws. These, while they exist in the mind as ideas, stand around us in nature forever embodied, a present sanity to expose and cure the insanity of men" (*EE*, "Nature," p. 400). The experimental character of Emerson's aesthetic sees nature as consequent to human perception, which contains within the mind "innate universal laws": "Nature is the incarnation of a thought, and turns to a thought, again, as ice becomes water and gas. The world is mind precipitated" (*EE*, "Nature," p. 400).

Idealism and dualism are obviously interwoven for Emerson, especially in the relationship between humanity and nature. According to Joel Porte, Emerson's idealism was "a simple denial of the inherent worth of matter and sense experience."[29] Instead of looking out, to nature, as in the work of Cage and Thoreau, Emerson saw nature as the symbolic embodiment of laws already written within the human mind: "For Emerson, then, love of life meant largely love of the eternal laws which he found symbolized by the phenomenal world. Things in themselves were dust and ashes."[30]

In his essay "Prudence" Emerson himself confirms Porte's point of view. Here, he compares two kinds of prudence, the first of which he calls "a base prudence, which is a devotion to matter, as if we possessed no other faculties than the palate, the nose, the touch, the eye and ear" (*EE*, pp. 158–159). The faculty most obviously omitted here is that of intellection. Emerson sees the intellect, functioning within the mind of humanity, as

capable of "true prudence." In so doing, he continues to emphasize the dualism he finds between inner and outer worlds, humanity and nature: "The true prudence limits this sensualism
by admitting the knowledge of an internal and real world" (EE,
p. 159). Emerson's "internal world" translates the outer world
of the senses through symbolism: "The world of the senses is
a world of shows; it does not exist for itself, but has a symbolic
character" (EE, p. 158).

Establishing a symbolical relationship between the real as
found in nature and the ideal as experienced by humanity is fundamental to what is known as transcendental correspondence.
As I have shown, Emerson saw humanity and nature as initially
separate and capable of being unified only through human effort.
He attempted such unification by using correspondence.[31] As
Joel Porte remarks, "Perhaps the most important idea that Emerson got from the eighteenth century is the notion of Correspondence: that nature is symbolic of spiritual truth, and that to be so
is, in fact, its highest and truest function."[32]

Emerson learned of correspondence through his readings
of the eighteenth-century mystic Emanuel Swedenborg.[33] And
it is this form of symbolism that permeates his conception of the
function of the artist in society. In his essay "The Poet," Emerson writes: "Nature offers all her creatures to him as a picture-
language. . . . Things admit of being used as symbols, because nature is a symbol, in the whole, and in every part" (EE, p. 269).
However, he suggests in this essay that it is the poet who arbi-
trates between such symbols and their expression: "Every man
should be so much an artist, that he could report in conversation
what had befallen him. Yet, in our experience, the rays or appul-
ses have sufficient force to arrive at the senses, but not enough
to reach the quick, and compel the reproduction of themselves
in speech. The poet is the person in whom these powers are in
balance, the man without impediment" (EE, p. 264). According
to Emerson, poetry exists at first within the ideal realm outside
that of experience. "Poetry was all written before time was,"
and it is the poet alone who is able to express it: "The poet is
the sayer, the namer, and represents beauty" (EE, p. 265, p. 264).
Such representation unifies real and ideal: "that the poet was or

could be one with his world," which, according to Roy Harvey Pearce, is the "manifest content" of "The Poet." That unification transforms experience into the realm of the "Oversoul": "For above all the essay makes it clear that Emerson as transcendental literary theorist had convinced himself that the poet, in 'receiving and imparting' the symbols of nature, transformed them into a 'new and higher fact,' a *single* fact, the One, the Oversoul, God."[34]

Although this book does not overtly concern the theological implications of "oneness," it does concern its impetus. For Emerson, it is the poet/artist who effects such "oneness" by connecting real and ideal. As Julie Ellison puts it, "Emerson grafts the doctrine of correspondence, which insists on the meaningful symbolic relation between image and idea, onto the theory of the metaphoric origins of language."[35] Relating image to idea has immense consequences in twentieth-century American poetry, which I will later address. In the area of musical aesthetics, the first American composer to transfer Emersonian correspondence from image to sound was Charles Ives. Ives did so through his use of extramusical references and his oft-cited use of musical quotation.

Extramusical references abound in his works. In the opinion of H. Wiley Hitchcock, "Like virtually every instrumental piece by Ives, it [the *Fourth Symphony*] arose out of so-called extramusical ideas; it has a 'programme.'"[36] Ives himself often described the program of a work. For example, he said of *Prelude and Postlude for a Thanksgiving Service:* "This was to represent the sternness and strength and austerity of the Puritan character, and it seemed to me that any of the major, minor, or diminished chords used alone gave too much a feeling of bodily ease, which the Puritan did not give in to."[37] Of another piece he explained, "*All the Way Around and Back* is but a trying to take off, in sounds and rhythms, a very common thing in a back lot—a foul ball—and the base runner on 3rd has to go all the way back to 1st."[38] According to Ives, a section of *Washington's Birthday* was meant to "give the picture of the dismal, bleak, cold weather of a February night near New Fairfield."[39] Finally, he wrote at length of his famous *Central Park in the Dark:*

This piece purports to be a picture-in-sounds of the sounds of nature and of happenings that men would hear some thirty or so years ago (before the combustion engine and radio monopolized the earth and air), when sitting on a bench in Central Park on a hot summer night. The strings represent the night sounds and silent darkness—interrupted by sounds [the rest of the orchestra] from the Casino over the pond— of street singers coming up from the Circle singing, in spots, the tunes of those days—of some "night owls" from Healy's whistling the latest or the Freshman March—the "occasional elevated," a street parade, or a "break-down" in the distance—of newsboys crying "uxtries"—of pianolas having a ragtime war in the apartment house "over the garden wall," a street car and a street band join in the chorus— a fire engine, a cab horse runs away, lands "over the fence and out," the wayfarers shout—again the darkness is heard —an echo over the pond—and we walk home.[40]

Ives's *Concord Sonata* is considered by some to be aesthetically the culminating work of his career. Howard Boatwright contends: "For some composers, one work, more than any other, may become a channel through which the streams of philosophical concept, musical technique, and style flow in singular unity. For Charles Ives, the *Concord Sonata* was such a work. It reflects programmatically, and also in deeper, less obvious ways, the influence of the Concord Transcendentalists" (*EB*, p. xiii). The *Essays* that were written to accompany the work have been and will continue to be cited in this book. They represent Ives's most detailed description of his mature aesthetic.

The composition itself contains excellent examples of both extramusical reference and quotation. For example, Ives wrote in the score about a passage in the *Emerson* movement:

This is but one of Emerson's sudden calls for a Transcendental Journey, which may be more widely reflected on p. 17. Chord in R.H. (3rd brace, page 17), three lowest notes A, B and C hit with thumb. In the chord at the end of the first measure, 5th brace, on this page, the lower D (L.H.) may be left out, the middle finger (L.H.) hitting the B natural and C, first finger the D, and the thumb striking the E and F in as strong and hard a way as possible, almost as though the Mountains of the Universe were shouting as all of Humanity rises to behold the "Massive Eternities" and the "Spiritual Immensities."[41]

However, one should note Ives's qualifier "almost" when attempting to imitate the "Mountains of the Universe." In the "Prologue" to his *Essays*, Ives addressed the issue of program music and the difference between defining what something *is* and recognizing the fluidity of how something *becomes:*

> [I]s not all music program music? Is not pure music, so called, representative in its essence? Is it not program music raised to the nth power, or, rather, reduced to the minus nth power? Where is the line to be drawn between the expression of subjective and objective emotion? It is easier to know *what* each is than when each *becomes* what it is. The 'Separateness of Art' theory—that art is not life, but a reflection of it, that art is not vital to life but that life is vital to it—does not help us. . . . Experiences are passed on from one man to another. . . . But where is the bridge placed—at the end of the road, or only at the end of our vision? Is it all a bridge, or is there no bridge because there is no gulf? (*EB*, "Prologue," pp. 4–5)

In this passage, it is Ives himself who refutes the opinions of those cited later who claim his quotations to be representational. Ives's approach to composition saw things in a process of "becoming." Art is not separate from life, nor is a bridge needed between one person's experience and another's. This was Ives's intention when he noted of his *Fourth of July:* "This is pure program music—it is also pure abstract music."[42] H. Wiley Hitchcock believes that "such dichotomies are inherent in Ives's music, and also in his thought about it."[43] In short, Ives expects the listener to consider neither abstraction nor the program separately, but to take them together as a whole.

However, there is a hierarchy attached to the importance Ives placed on program versus abstraction. He maintained that the movements of his *Holidays Symphony* "make pictures in music of common events in the lives of common people . . . they could be played as abstract music (giving no titles [or] program), and then they would be just like all other 'abstract' things in art—one of two things: a covering up, or ignorance of (or but a vague feeling of) the human something at its source."[44] The program behind the music was more important to Ives than the sonic result. The "human something at its source" is what is most valuable, and it is this distinction that informs what is arguably his most famous remark: "My God! What has sound got to do with music!" (*EB*, "Epilogue," p. 84). Ives wrote that "in working these sound-pictures out (or trying to), it gave the ears plenty of new sound experiences."[45] This establishes the order in which Ives worked; the "sound-pictures" (that is, the program) came first. This process of translating extramusical ideas into musical sounds is what "gave the ears plenty of new sound experiences." Rosalie Sandra Perry has observed that "Ives' practice of musical quotation spans his whole work."[46] He saw the issue not as how the extramusical reference resonated either socially or historically but as how the reference came to mean something *within* the self. Concerning Ives's use of quotation, Perry remarks: "His imagery grows out of the essential character of the quoted tune, but the imagery carries with it as a corollary a mass of memories."[47] As I will point out, it is that "mass of memories" resonating within both Ives's use of extramusical references and his use of musical quotation that will constitute his continuation of Emersonian correspondence.[48]

Ives's critics have often misunderstood his use of quotation. John Cage, for example, regarded it as a reference to nationalism:

> [T]he American aspects of his music strike me as, endearing and touching and sentimental as they are, they strike me as the part of his work that is not basically interesting. If one is going to have referential material like that, I would be happier if it was global in extent rather than specific to one country as is the referential material of Ives' music.[49]

Elliott Carter, another composer critical of this aspect of Ives's music, has commented that he was

> perplexed at times by the disturbing lack of musical and stylistic continuity, caused largely by the constant use of musical quotations in many works. To me a composer develops his own personal language, suitable to express his field of experience and thought. When he borrows music from another style and thought from his own, he is admitting that he did not really experience what he is presenting but has to borrow from someone else who did. . . . It is, to me, disappointing that Ives too frequently was unable or unwilling to invent musical material that expressed his own vision authentically, instead of relying on the material of others.[50]

Both Cage and Carter object to Ives's quotations as involving content rather than form. Frank Rossiter has observed that Ives's "distinction [between substance and manner] was not unlike the more familiar dualism between content and form."[51] Most of what Ives considered as "substance" concerns musical content. For example, in the "Hawthorne" chapter of his *Essays*, Ives described the music as "not something that happens, but the way something happens" (*EB*, p. 42). This is usually cited as an example (and it is a good one) of Ives's emphasis on process. As such, it has sometimes confused the issue by suggesting, as Larry Starr writes, that the music "may be heard as quotations of *styles*. Their function is a formal one."[52] However, in the context of this discussion, I wish to draw attention to the use of the word "something." In Ives's music there is always a "something" present; this "something," when it involves his idea of substance, is always content-based rather than formal. Speaking about "In the Night" (the third movement of *Set for Theatre Orchestra*), Ives described this distinction: "Behind the music is a simpler picture—the heart of an old man, dying alone in the night, sad, low in heart—then God comes to help him—bring him to his own loved ones. This is the main line, the substance."[53]

Cage and Carter see Ives's quotations as borrowed from

outside experiences, as if they were examples of a representational approach to artmaking. J. Peter Burkholder, in fact, uses this point of view to reject the opinion that the music of Ives is Transcendentalist in nature. As Burkholder sees it, the principal aim of Ives, in the "works of his maturity," was "the representation in music of human experience."[54] He later explains that such representation, and "the larger concept of imitation," was in direct opposition to the transcendentalists: "In writing representational music, even music about the spiritual questing of Emerson and the contemplation of Thoreau, Ives was pursuing aims entirely in conflict with this aspect of Transcendentalist thought."[55]

I regard Ives's musical quotations as more than formal or representational. For Ives, form has to do with what he disdained as "manner." Aligning himself with Emerson, he sought to disengage the necessity of meter as form in favor of the "metremaking argument" of content (*EE*, "The Poet," p. 266). It is content, the "substance" of his quotations, that is of interest here, and his use of quotation goes beyond the notion of merely representing outside experience.[56]

For Ives, such experience was transformed as it entered the creative mind of the artist. It is this transformation that moves away from the use of quotation as a kind of representational art. It also contradicts Rosalie Sandra Perry's view that the "exactness and universality of representation of Ives' realism assumes the form of quoted tunes."[57] Ives's quotations are not "exact" at all; they are, instead, his *memory* of those experiences.[58]

It is through memory that Ives achieved transcendental correspondence in music, connecting himself and the beginnings of twentieth-century American experimental music with the literary tradition of Emerson. Ives's memories are the "substance" of his quotations in particular and of his music as a whole. According to H. Wiley Hitchcock, Ives's quotations were "audible expressions of his transcendentalist conviction that 'all occupations of man's body and soul in their diversity come from but one mind and soul!' This sense of the oneness of human experience, of the immanence of an Emersonian oversoul in all things, everyday and commonplace as well as highly artful, is accomplished concretely by Ives through his choice of musical materials, his perception of interrelatedness among them, and his fusion of them into a new and convincing synthesis."[59]

This is at the heart of Ives's continuation of Emersonian correspondence, symbolizing not what was observed but a translation of the observation into something else: a symbol of that something that corresponds to the memory of what happened rather than its actual occurrence. In his essay on Emerson, Ives remarked that "[n]ature loves analogy and hates repetition" (*EB*, "Emerson," p. 22).[60] Even though Ives seems to be quoting Emerson here, as is frequently the case there is apparently no exactly corresponding passage in any of Emerson's writings. This is in keeping with the disdain for repetition Ives expresses in the sentence. It also parallels how he used quotations in his musical works; there, too, they are rarely exact repetitions.

In his *Concord Sonata*, Ives uses Beethoven's "epic motif" (from the *Fifth Symphony*) in a variety of ways. As Henry Cowell puts it, "Almost every conceivable type of variation is applied to the epic motif."[61] H. Wiley Hitchcock notes that in the *Concord Sonata* Beethoven's motif shares a common pitch-pattern with two hymn tunes, *Missionary Chant* and *Martyn*. "Ives makes clear in *Concord* that he has all three sources in mind by quoting them separately and integrally. . . . Ultimately, one perceives that all the thematic materials of the sonata relate to one another. . . . Thus does the network of musical inter-relationships and of extra-musical associations broaden, to make for a transcendental unity in the *Concord Sonata*."[62] And the connection that enables such unity to occur are the memories, musical and otherwise, that fueled the creative mind of Charles Ives.

Through memory, Charles Ives internalized and transformed his experiences into musical results symbolizing the relationship between that experienced reality and its idealized compositional form. As Rosalie Sandra Perry observes, "When music draws heavily upon existing material, as in the quotations of Ives, such music possesses an internal symbolism."[63] The correspondence between experienced reality and Ives's idealized memory of it is the aesthetic "substance" of his compositional work. In the view of Larry Starr, "It is Ives's substance that seems to so elude the search for obvious sources of influence."[64] If his "substance" has eluded any traces of influence, it is because of the necessity of knowing more about the importance of literary influences on Ives. Transcendentalism is that influence and it manifests itself as "substance" in Ives via transcendental correspondence.

Betty E. Ch'maj remarks that "[i]t is in music more than in any other art, as we are now beginning to discover, that Emersonian ideas seem to carry into our own time and speak to the modern world."[65] By fusing actual experience and idealized memory into a musical form, Ives continued both Emersonian idealism and the controlling self's imposition of unity upon initially dual experience. It is this that separates his musical aesthetics from those of his experimental successor, John Cage.[66]

NONDUALISM AND COEXISTENCE

Henry David Thoreau and John Cage

Homme, libre penseur! te crois-tu seul pensant
Dans ce monde où la vie éclate en toute chose?
[Man, free thinker! do you imagine you think alone
In this world where life bursts forth in all things?]
—Gérard de Nerval ("Vers dorés")

As the ocean so mysterious rolls toward me closer and closer,
I too but signify at the utmost a little wash'd-up drift,
A few sands and dead leaves to gather,
Gather, and merge myself as part of the sands and drift.
—Walt Whitman ("As I Ebb'd with the Ocean of Life")

Henry David Thoreau and John Cage depart from the experimental aesthetic views of Emerson and Ives in the following ways. First, they see humanity's relation to the world as nondualistic. Their experiments do not require human imposition; they simply require attentive observation. Second, Thoreau and Cage do not practice the tenets of philosophical idealism; since humanity and nature are not separate, reality is not twofold and dual. Observation need not be interpreted; one may instead seek to discover things "as they are." Thoreau and Cage experiment without presupposed hypotheses. Their version of experience is nondual; ideal and real do not need human reconciliation.

Thoreau's two-year residence at Walden Pond is his most famous experiment, an "experiment of living":

> I went to the woods because I wished to live deliberately, to front only the essential facts of life, and see if I could not learn what it had to teach, and not, when I came to die, discover that I had not lived. I did not wish to live what was not life, living is so dear; nor did I wish to practise resignation, unless it was quite necessary. I wanted to live deep and suck out all the marrow of life, to live so sturdily and Spartan-like as to put to rout all that was not life, to cut a broad swath and shave close, to drive life into a corner, and reduce it to its lowest terms, and, if it proved to be mean, why then to get the whole and genuine meanness of it, and publish its meanness to the world; or if it were sublime, to know it by experience, and be able to give a true account of it in my next excursion. For most men, it appears to me, are in a strange uncertainty about it, whether it is of the devil or of God, and have *somewhat hastily* concluded that it is the chief end of man here to "glorify God and enjoy him forever."[1]

I cite this famous passage at length to demonstrate the open-ended nature of the Walden experiment. First, the experiment did not begin with a hypothesis but with a question: what is and is not life? Thoreau wrote about his experiment without the preconditions that normally inform a hypothesis. He emphasized disinterested observation, rather than comparing humanly predetermined conceptions with those discovered experimentally.[2] In other words, Thoreau had no expectations of what he might find. Equally important is this passage's stance concerning value judgments. It is presumed that Thoreau will accept his discoveries regardless of the outcome. Truth is not ideally pre-existent; it is, instead, experientially present.

Thus, Thoreau rejected the *a priori* acceptance of idealism. Even the metaphysical, if it is to exist at all, must be discovered through experience.[3] The self does not mediate between physical and metaphysical worlds. In his experiment at Walden Pond, Thoreau sought to establish his place solely within the physical world. In the "Prospects" chapter of *Nature* (his first book), Emerson advised: "Build therefore your own world. As fast as you conform your life to the pure idea in your mind, that will unfold its great proportions."[4] In contrast, Thoreau wished to discover the world as it is, not as the human mind conceives of and shapes it. That, in fact, was his experiment.[5]

For John Cage, experiment was equally open-ended. In 1955, he commented that "the word 'experimental' is apt, providing it is understood not as descriptive of an act to be later judged in terms of success and failure, but simply as of an act the outcome of which is unknown."[6] This was not always the case. Earlier in his career, he saw composition quite differently.

> Formerly, whenever anyone said the music I presented was experimental, I objected. It seemed to me that composers knew what they were doing, and that the experiments that had been made had taken place prior to the finished works, just as sketches are made before paintings and rehearsals precede performances. . . .
>
> Now, on the other hand, times have changed; music has changed; and I no longer object to the word "experimental." I use it in fact to describe all the music that especially interests me and to which I am devoted, whether someone else wrote it or I myself did. What has happened is that I have become a listener and the music has become something to hear. (*S*, "Experimental Music," p. 7)

Whereas he used to see experiments as preparations for a completed work (as Thoreau's journals might be viewed as preparations for *Walden*), Cage had begun to see the experiment itself as the work of art. Essential to that change was his re-evaluation of the composer's role. He had become a "listener," with the implication that once experimental means are established the ends will take care of themselves. In fact, whether a work ends is really not the issue. It is the listener's attention that determines such parameters, involving as it does the simple observation of whatever happens without expectations (which is remarkably similar to the way in which Thoreau often wrote journal entries).

Cage's approach to writing music radically alters the composer's place in the compositional process. By the mid-1950s (when he wrote the passages cited above), Cage had stopped exercising total control over how he wrote music. As a composer, he was no longer the single creative force behind a piece. The experimental work had ceased being an object and had instead become the process of its occurrence. Cage himself was simply a part of that process.

Like Thoreau, Cage disapproved of philosophical idealism. He long spoke against correspondences between physical experience and metaphysical meanings.[7] For example, one of the central issues of Cage's work was his wish to put an end to extramusical references. This is initiated by composers who remove their intellectual control over sound and let the sounds *be* sounds: "Something more far-reaching is necessary: a composing of sounds within a universe predicated upon the sounds themselves rather than upon the mind which can envisage their coming into being" (S, "Composition as Process," pp. 27–28). However, since the composer, according to Cage, has become a listener, it is not just the process of making that removes such controls; the method of perception removes control as well. Thus, the result is a way of making that is grounded in listening; a listening that brings no expectations to the sounds other than allowing them to simply be: "Why should they imagine that sounds are not interesting in themselves? I'm always amazed when people say, 'Do you mean it's just sounds?' How they can imagine that it's anything but sounds is what's so mysterious."[8] It requires "imagination" to make references between sounds and extramusical meanings and that is one instance of Cage's disapproval. For imagination, as part of a human self that interprets rather than observes, is what fuels the idealism of things corresponding to meanings that exist apart from their physical realities.

Cage's rejection of idealism, and his desire to experience rather than interpret the unknown, was a sign of his wish to make art free of the control of his intentions. One should not infer, as some do, that this means Cage was able to free the work of his intentions altogether. It is the *control* of intention, and its denial of non-intention's existence, that Cage wished to expel from the process of making. Control assumes a hierarchical relationship between nature and humanity that disallows the presence of what we do not intend. Cage's move toward non-intention was an attempt to remove such separations: "If, at this point, one says, 'Yes! I do not discriminate between intention and non-intention,' the splits, subject-object, art-life, etc., disappear" (S, "Experimental Music: Doctrine," p. 14). For Cage, accepting and appreciating the unintentional resulted in a nondualistic approach to reality. The analysis that follows will demonstrate that Thoreau shared many of Cage's views, including an acceptance and appreciation of the unintentional. It will also show, by describing the unopposed nature of sound and silence, that the "reconciliation of opposites" is unnecessary to either Cage or Thoreau. Both of these views are grounded in a nondual universe, where humanity and nature are not separate, where coexistence replaces control—where there is no need for reconciliation because there are no opposites.

THOREAU

The experimentalism of Henry David Thoreau differed significantly from Emerson's. The older man's experimentalism had a fixed hypothesis, seeking to discover inherent truths in nature that would correspond to human concerns. And, as discussed in the last chapter, since humanity and nature are separate and only unified by the human act of reconciliation, nature's importance was determined in relation to humanity, the source of unification. For Emerson, humanity remained at the center of discourse; thus, the direction of his experiment was toward humanity.

Thoreau sought to discover the human place in nature, not nature's place in humanity. Humanity and nature were not separate: "All beauty, all music, all delight springs from apparent dualism but real unity."[9] This "real unity" is not forged by human consciousness; it already exists. It is our human conception of separateness that is faulty. And it is the idea of concepts themselves that, as Emerson notes, "apprizes us of a dualism."[10] To discover "real unity" necessitated movement from conception (human interpretation) to perception (human observation). In so doing, Thoreau developed an approach to writing that moved away from correspondences between perceptions and conceptions, between observed experiences and humanly conceived meanings. He instead began to write as a medium rather than as an explicator.[11] It calls to mind the shift of knowledge that took place when Copernican theory proved that the sun, not the earth, was at the center of our solar system. We were part of, but not central to, what was around us. This paradigmatic shift, transferred from physics to literature, is a movement away from the Emersonian self. It is a shift away from the creative self as the separated center of discourse toward a creative self that is a coexistent part of the discourse. For Thoreau, engendering that creative self necessitated a movement toward nature.[12]

I contend that this movement toward nature characterizes Thoreau's entire body of work. How then does one reconcile this with the writing of *Walden,* an extremely well conceived work of art where the self is so clearly the central character: "I should not talk so much about myself if there were anybody else whom I knew as well" (*W,* "Economy," p. 3). Joel Porte, whose *Emerson and Thoreau* was an early example of criticism in favor of Thoreau as a distinctive voice, takes the title of his book *In Respect to Egotism*[13] from *Walden:* "In most books, the *I,* or first person, is omitted; in this it will be retained; that, in respect to egotism, is the main difference" (*W,* "Economy," p. 3). Thus, even those critics who see Emerson and Thoreau as distinct rather than connected only rarely question the primacy of the creative self in

Thoreau's writing.[14] Where and how, then, does Thoreau's movement toward nature de-center the self?

Let me begin with a question frequently addressed by Thoreau scholars: Is *Walden* the completed masterwork of which the *Journal* is but mere source material? Or is the *Journal* primary and *Walden* an act of communication between Thoreau and his audience, where Thoreau plays the part of the chanticleer "waking his neighbors up," in the common parlance of his and (to a large extent still) our time (*W*, "Where I Lived and What I Lived For," p. 76)? I believe, along with such scholars as Sharon Cameron, Perry Miller, and Walter Harding, that the *Journal* is indeed the primary text. But I also believe that *Walden* is the road map that leads to the *Journal*; that the direction begins with humanity, both the neighbors written to and the author writing initially in the role of the Emersonian self—a self recognizably accepted in that historical time. However, I see *Walden* moving away from the self as central to written discourse, a movement that culminates at the end of the book. *Walden* leads the way to a re-examination of the role of the self by moving toward a view of nature that sees humanity as a part of it rather than in control of it. In what follows, I will show how *Walden* progressively shifts from the separate human centeredness of Emerson toward a more integrated view of humanity in the world.

The opening of *Walden* (already cited) points to an author who is clearly the protagonist of this tale, its hero, if you will. Thoreau had a Harvard education grounded in the classics. He was particularly taken by the Greeks and frequently quoted from Homer's *Iliad*. Thoreau was quite aware of the historical significance of writing in the guise of a hero describing the journey of the hero's quest. But what kind of hero? Western heroes often exhibit elements of the tragic; from Prometheus to Oedipus, the emphasis is on human transcendence in the face of disastrous circumstances. Is this the heroic journey that Thoreau is describing? I think not. Instead, I believe he was the kind of hero John Cage wrote about in his "Lecture on Something": "The mythological and Oriental view of the hero is the one who accepts life" (*S*, p. 134). Such acceptance is at the heart of the coexistent aesthetic I see in the work of both Thoreau and his twentieth-century disciple John Cage. It is a movement away from the centered human consciousness that informs Descartes's "I think therefore I am," sees its continuance in Emersonian and Ivesian thought, and represents well what Cage objects to when he asserts that "trying to force life into one's own idea of it, of what it should be, is only absurd" (S, "Lecture on Something," p. 134).

I see *Walden*, Thoreau's heroic journey, directed toward disentangling the serpentine hold our human perspective brings to experience. How does he begin? First, by prying away all that seems superfluous. And, starting with "Economy," what is superfluous is almost inevitably humanly constructed. Two superfluities merit special consideration here. First, both past and future are constructs; they are humanly constructed because they are not directly experienced. The past, that which is either previously experienced or preserved by some recording means, exists solely in the realm of human memory. The future, that which has never been experienced and exists only speculatively in the human imagination, is like the carrot dangling in front of the workhorse; tantalizing, yes, but unreachable lest it appear in the present, and the future become something else. Thoreau observed of these issues: "I have been anxious to improve the nick of time, and notch it on my stick too; to stand on the meeting of two eternities, the past and future, which is precisely the present moment; to toe that line" (W, "Economy," p. 15). Human experience, as finite as the looming fact of imminent death, cannot fathom eternity, and, this being the case, Thoreau is thus describing an acceptance of the reality of human existence, apart from the idealized conceptions of either past or future.

And what, in Thoreau's view, exemplified the perpetuity of the present better than nature? To coexist in nature's presence, to attempt to experience the reality of nature as it happened, was for him to bring humanity into right relation, not as a separate interpreter of experience, but as an integral part of that experience: "To anticipate, not the sunrise and the dawn merely, but, if possible, Nature herself!" (W, "Economy," p. 15). And how did one begin to participate in such a way? "It is true, I never as-sisted the sun materially in his rising, but, doubt not, it was of the last importance only to be present at it" (*W*, "Economy," pp. 15–16).

It would be reductive in the extreme to suggest that as Thoreau moves toward nature, which I believe these citations suggest, the self is diminished. I do not see his journey as self-immolation, a phoenix-like artistic mission that results in a renewed and immortal self. Instead, I see Thoreau's journey as a perceptive look outside the self, undertaken in such a way as to afford one the ability to see the self as coexistent with what is perceived. *Walden* may still be viewed as a symbolic work of ex-traordinary magnitude; indeed, critics have spent entire careers explicating such analogous meanings. I, however, find some-thing else at play. When Thoreau writes admiringly of primitive man as "but a sojourner in nature" (*W*, "Economy," p. 33) he is describing humanity and nature as having coexistent status. This status, he admonishes, has been lost: "But lo! men have be-come the tools of their tools" (*W*, "Economy," p. 33). The direc-tion implied is away from human contrivance. Likewise, his vi-sion of art (he clearly knows that his vision is an artistic one) is directed, even in the earliest passages of *Walden*, toward nature and away from such human controls: "We have built for this world a family mansion, and for the next a family tomb. The best works of art are the expression of man's struggle to free him-self from this condition, but the effect of our art is merely to make this low state comfortable and that higher state to be for-gotten" (*W*, "Economy," p. 33).

What may seem at first to be self-immolation is, instead, a clearing-away process. This allows room for the presence of what seems to exist apart from the self but is, instead, inseparably part of the self: "Before we can adorn our houses with beautiful ob-jects the walls must be stripped, and our lives must be stripped, and beautiful housekeeping and beautiful living be laid for a foundation: now, a taste for the beautiful is most cultivated out of doors, where there is no house and no housekeeper" (*W*, "Economy," p. 34). In other words, the coexistent life experience, where self and nature are shared rather than separate, initially requires a looking outward; only by looking toward nature and away from the self can one see that there is anything other than the self to begin with. This is the real significance of Thoreau's residence at Walden. His independence, which begins when he arrives (on the Fourth of July!), is not just from social convention—it is also from the dominance of *all* human convention.

This is decidedly unlike Emerson. In "Man the Reformer," he saw the world as incomplete and proclaimed the role of humanity to be its unifier, its completer, its reformer:

> What is a man born for but to be a Reformer, a Re-maker of what man has made; a renouncer of lies; a restorer of truth and good, imitating that great Nature which embosoms us all, and which sleeps no moment on an old past, but every hour repairs herself, yielding us every morning a new day, and with every pulsation a new life? Let him renounce everything which is not true to him, and put all his practices back on their first thoughts, and do nothing for which he has not the whole world for his reason.[15]

Here nature is described as humanity's tool for restoring truth, and it is no surprise that in the same essay Emerson writes of economy as "a high, humane office, a sacrament, when its aim is grand."[16]

Thoreau seeks the world as it is, complete in itself. In his own chapter entitled "Economy" he describes the reformer as having an ailment: "If anything ail a man, so that he does not perform his functions . . . he forthwith sets about reforming— the world" (*W*, p. 69). Thoreau's task, unlike Emerson's, is not a human reforming of the world as it "should" be; it is, instead, the actual discovery of the world as it is. Instead of using the natural world to prove an internally created conception of the world, Thoreau looked outward, in an experiment at Walden that held no predetermined hypothesis: "for I found myself suddenly neighbor to the birds; not by having imprisoned one, but having caged myself near them" (*W*, "Where I Lived and What I Lived

For," p. 77). Rather than alter the world to meet human con-ceptions (that is, imprisoning the bird), Thoreau chose instead to "cage," to alter, himself by examining the world on its own terms. The results? "Shams and delusions are esteemed for soundest truths, while reality is fabulous. If men would steadily observe realities only, and not allow themselves to be deluded, life, to compare it with such things as we know, would be like a fairy tale" (W, "Where I Lived and What I Lived For," p. 86).[17]

It is at this critical point in Thoreau's text that those who wish to align him with Emerson stake their claim. Thoreau writes, "The universe constantly and obediently answers to our conceptions" (W, "Where I Lived and What I Lived For," p. 87). Stanley Cavell, in his book *The Senses of Walden*, believes this statement corresponds to the idea of *a priori* truths—that is, pre-existent knowledge within the self that can be confirmed by natural experience. Further, and even more important to this analysis, he aligns such a statement with the Emersonian idea of "building your own world":[18] "We *are* creating the world, heaven is under our feet as well as over our heads—however much of it we have placed. The universe constantly and obediently answers to our conceptions" (SW, p. 112). However, Cavell, who leaves *Walden* in search of Emerson (where he more rightfully explores his own philosophical views), takes Thoreau's remarks out of context. Such conceptions can only be found when one is im-mersed in nature. In other words, when humanity and nature coexist without separations, our conceptions are met by natu-ral perceptions; our thoughts no longer interpret but are instead equal to our perceptions:

> Men esteem truth remote, in the outskirts of the system, behind the farthest star, before Adam and after the last man. In eternity there is indeed something true and sublime. But all these times and places and occasions are now and here. God himself culminates in the present moment, and will never be more divine in the lapse of all the ages. And we are enabled to apprehend at all what is sublime and noble only by the perpetual instilling and drenching of the reality that

surrounds us. The universe constantly and obediently answers to our conceptions; whether we travel fast or slow, the track is laid for us. (*W*, "Where I Lived and What I Lived For," p. 87)

Thoreau placed the ideal in the here and now; real and ideal are the same experience, and eternity exists in the present moment. These conditions are not ideally constructed by the human spirit, a reforming of experience; they are, instead, when one is in direct contact with "reality," actual experiences. And while Thoreau did indeed mention that the universe answers to our conceptions, he finished that remark by saying "the track is laid for us." According to Thoreau, conception is not *a priori* in the self; it is experientially discovered in nature by means of human perception. This is essentially opposite the Emersonian view of the poet found in the "Idealism" chapter of *Nature:* "The sensual man conforms thoughts to things; the poet conforms things to his thoughts. The one esteems nature as rooted and fast; the other, as fluid, and impresses his being thereon."[19] This statement, previously cited, clarifies the distinction I make between Emerson and Thoreau. Emerson's poet constructs reality by conforming external to internal; the creative self intentionally takes control, shaping natural reality by "impressing his being thereon."

Thoreau, on the other hand, is not so easily pigeonholed as being a "sensual man." He was not "conforming" thoughts to things by looking outward. Nor is it nature rather than (according to Emerson at least) humanity that is fixed. For Thoreau, such conclusions speak of a duality not found in experience. Neither humanity nor nature is fixed; neither do thoughts and things conform to one or the other. Both exist in the same plane, and it is this nondual version of experience that makes up what Thoreau considered to be reality. And though *Walden* is his attempt to communicate that reality to his "neighbors," it is in his *Journal* where we find his experience of that reality. In *Walden*, as John Cage notes, we find the answer to the question "Is life worth living?"[20] In his *Journal*, as Sharon Cameron notes, questions remain questions. *Walden* is a communicated response to experience; the *Journal* is simply the record of his experience.[21]

However, the progression of *Walden* is also at variance with an internally constructed Emersonian self. The movement away from a controlling self and toward an experience of coexistence with nature manifests itself continually throughout the book. Consider these lines from "Solitude": "This is a delicious evening, when the whole body is one sense, and imbibes delight through every pore. I go and come with a strange liberty in Nature, a part of herself" (*W*, p. 117). Such musing shares, to some degree, the sentiment of Emerson's "transparent eyeball": "the currents of the Universal Being circulate through me."[22] Once again, however, it is the direction that differs. For Emerson, the "Universal Being" flows through *him*, whereas for Thoreau the affinity is outward; he feels as if he is a part of nature, instead of feeling as if nature resides within.

This may, for those familiar with Cavell, seem akin to what he sees in *Walden* as neighboring: "What is next to us is what we neighbor. The writer [Thoreau] has spoken of finding himself suddenly neighbor to the birds. . . . Our relation to nature, at its best, would be that of neighboring it—knowing the grandest laws it is executing, while nevertheless 'not wholly involved in them'" (*SW*, p. 105). What is implied here is separation; a neighboring that does indeed place humanity "next to" nature as it, nonetheless, stands apart. Taken out of context, Cavell's point has merit. But, if one considers the actual words of Thoreau outside the context prepared by Cavell, a different picture emerges.

I have already mentioned the caged-bird passage, in which I suggested that Thoreau "caged" himself, that he was involved in a process of self- rather than world-alteration. This constitutes an example of Thoreau's reversal of Emersonian ideas by moving in the direction of nature rather than in that of humanity. Cavell takes his position of neighboring as allowing for the "condition of 'having' a self, and knowing it" (*SW*, p. 104). He then cites Thoreau: "Nearest to all things is that power which fashions their being. *Next* to us the grandest laws are continually being executed. *Next* to us is not the workman whom we have hired, with whom we love so well to talk, but the workman whose work we are" (*W*, "Solitude," p. 121). First and foremost in relation to my discussion here is the distinction Thoreau makes: "*Next* to us is not the workman whom we have hired." Clearly this neighbor is not constructed by us. On the other hand, that does not assume separation. We are the work of that "workman," and, as such, there is a connection between us.

One more omission from Cavell's account is what comes after:

> "How vast and profound is the influence of the subtile powers of Heaven and of Earth! We seek to perceive them, and we do not see them; we seek to hear them, and we do not hear them; identified with the substance of things, they cannot be separated from them. They cause that in all the universe men purify and sanctify their hearts, and clothe themselves in their holiday garments to offer sacrifices and oblations to their ancestors. It is an ocean of subtile intelligences. They are everywhere, above us, on our left, on our right; they environ us on all sides." (*W*, "Solitude," pp. 121–122)

Seeking cannot uncover heaven and earth because they are not separate from the substance of things. True neighboring, in Thoreau's words rather than Cavell's, is not a recovery of a separate sense of self resulting from the discovery of something "other" or "next to." It is, instead, the realization that the coexistence of self and nature is not separate at all. Thoreau himself suggests as much when he continues: "With thinking we may be beside ourselves in a sane sense. By a conscious effort of the mind we can stand aloof from actions and their consequences; and all things, good and bad, go by us like a torrent. We are not wholly involved in Nature. I may be either the driftwood in the stream, or Indra in the sky looking down on it" (*W*, "Solitude," p. 122).

The context is completely missing when Cavell remarks that "we are not wholly involved" in nature. Separation is characterized by thinking, "by a conscious effort of the mind." For Thoreau our natural state or condition, before the conception of thought, our perception of "reality" harkening back to an earlier passage, is not separate; it is nondual. Looking toward nature, away from the Emersonian self, leads one to the realization that nature and humanity are not separate at all. Nondualism may be a radical departure from nineteenth-century romanticism. However, it is entirely consistent with an Asian view of reality. Thus, it is enlightening to note that the passage where Thoreau writes of the nonseparation between idealism, "the powers of Heaven and of Earth," and reality, "the substance of things," has quotation marks around it. As Walter Harding notes in *The Variorum "Walden,"* Thoreau is quoting Confucius.[23]

Thoreau's recognition of the nondual nature of human experience resulted in a work that moves away from a written self as the exclusive center of experience toward a more inclusive method of writing that sees the self as but part of experience. At the end of *Walden,* Thoreau continued to emphasize that direction: "the universe is wider than our views of it" (*W*, "Conclusion," p. 285). Given that understanding, Thoreau could then, with such perspective, suggest "Explore thyself" (*W*, "Conclusion," p. 287), re-establishing a consideration of the self in the context of a world that extends beyond that self.

Thoreau's exploration extended beyond the rational, beyond the knowable: "It is a ridiculous demand which England and America make, that you shall speak so that they can understand you. Neither men nor toadstools grow so. As if that were important, and there were not enough to understand you without them. As if Nature could support but one order of understandings, could not sustain birds as well as quadrupeds, flying as well as creeping things" (*W*, "Conclusion," pp. 288–289). This departs from what Cavell calls an "epistemology of conscience" with an "emphasis upon listening and answering" (*SW*, p. 88). Throughout *Walden,* Thoreau moves more and more toward listening without answering. It is significant that the chapter entitled "Sounds" ends as follows: "Instead of no path to the front-yard gate in the Great Snow,—no gate—no front-yard,—and no path to the civilized world" (*W*, p. 116). Listening without answering leads one away from the humanly conceived boundaries of knowledge, understanding, and epistemology.

Throughout his criticism of *Walden*, Cavell imposes his own "sense" rather than Thoreau's. *Walden* is not a quest "for the recovery of the self, as from an illness" (*SW*, p. 80). As I have pointed out, its author showed great disdain for such attempts at recovery and reform. Instead, Thoreau wished to move away from epistemological concerns, to step beyond human understanding and the human boundaries of knowledge: "I desire to speak somewhere *without* bounds; like a man in a waking moment, to men in their waking moments" (*W*, "Conclusion," p. 289). When we are awake, Thoreau implies, there are no boundaries, no separations. His quest is not the recovery of the self from illness but the realization of health through acceptance.

Thoreau did not share the negative view that the world was unacceptable and needed, by human means, to be reformed. Rather than attempt, by reconciliation, to unify self and world, Thoreau offered the nondual view that the world includes us and is already unified, thus putting an end to the conceit that our universe is somehow dependent upon us for completion. Cavell himself suggests as much:

> But there is a recurrent form of doubt about Thoreau's writing which may threaten the balance of any of my deliberations with his book and thereby take the heart out of the reader's efforts to try it further. The form of doubt is caused partly by the depth of the book's depressions and the height of its elevations, and, more nearly, by the absence of reconciliation between them, which may seem evasive or irresolute of the writer—as if we have been led once more only to the limits of one man's willingness to answer, not to limits of the humanly answerable. (*SW*, p. 110)

This possibility, that Thoreau did not reconcile the heights and depths of experience, should not "take the heart out of the reader's efforts to try it further." It is, instead, the very reason *Walden* continues to be readable. By the end of the book, one discovers that there are no answers—that what makes Thoreau such an interesting writer are the questions he asks. It would really have been irresponsible had Thoreau presumed, like many of his critics then and now, that the questions he asked were or are ever answerable. On the other hand, neither is this (as Sharon Cameron suggests) a tragic vision where questions cannot be answered because nature as "other" can only be observed, not known.[24] Instead, I see Thoreau's unanswered questions more optimistically. He goes neither just inside, as Cavell has it, or just outside, as Sharon Cameron suggests. Thoreau moved toward nature in order to gain perspective, and it was an experiment that attempted to discover what role the self plays within nature. What he found was nondualism; there is no "other."

Once Thoreau had determined the nondual relationship between humanity and nature, he could, as he does at the end of *Walden*, return to the self. This is somewhat similar to John Cage's description of Zen: "Before studying Zen, men are men and mountains are mountains. While studying Zen, things get confused. After studying Zen, men are men and mountains are mountains. No difference except that one is no longer attached" (*S*, "Lecture on Something," p. 143). What happens after Zen is that distinctions of self and other no longer apply and our attachment to them disappears.

John Cage closes the introduction to his Norton Lectures with these remarks: "In the nature of the use of chance operations is the belief that all answers answer all questions. The nonhomogeneity that characterizes the source material of these lectures suggests that anything says what you have to say, that meaning is in the breath, that without thinking we can tell what is being said without understanding it."[25] Thoreau ends *Walden* with a remarkably similar statement: "I do not say that John or Jonathan will realize all this; but such is the character of that morrow which mere lapse of time can never make to dawn. The light which puts out our eyes is darkness to us. Only that day dawns to which we are awake. There is more day to dawn. The sun is but a morning star" (*W*, "Conclusion," p. 297). Opposites are not opposites; all answers answer all questions; what seems to be darkness is really light; suns are really stars. These are non-dual perceptions and comprise, in large part, the reason Cage so admired Thoreau. He believed that Thoreau shared his nondual view of reality; that being awake, for Thoreau, was the ability to, without thinking, be able to "tell what is being said without understanding it."

CAGE AND THOREAU

Had Cage never read Thoreau, he might have remained a "musical outsider," relegated to an important position in the midst of a group of other distinguished outsiders known under the aegis of the "American Experimental Tradition." As previously discussed, Charles Ives, the "father of American music" and founding member of such musical experimentalism, discovered his musical lineage among the literary geniuses of Concord. By aligning himself with Thoreau, Cage took his place alongside Ives as a truly representative "American" composer. And yet, although Ives seems to be making his way into the American musical canon, Cage, at least in the United States, maintains his "outsider" status.

Jonathan Brent has observed that "Cage's work cannot be assessed from the standpoint of traditional aesthetics." Later in the same piece, however, he remarks that "[i]n Europe he is seen as characteristically American; in America he is seen as an anomaly."[26] Is this a paradox? By answering yes to that question, one is able to place Thoreau in an equally paradoxical position. Cage's opinion of him takes Thoreau decidedly out of the Western aesthetic tradition as well. If Cage was right, does that somehow remove Thoreau from the American literary canon? Or does it open the way for Cage to enter the American musical canon?

I would suggest that Europe has a much clearer sense of what is "American" than does the U.S. musical establishment. Cage wrote the words "Reading Thoreau's *Journal*, I discover any idea I've ever had worth its salt" as an invitation.[27] If he was right, as I intend to prove in the following analysis, scholars might well have to open a new channel in the mainstream of American music, making room for that so-called iconoclast John Cage.

In his "Lecture on Nothing," Cage proclaimed: "I have nothing to say and I am saying it and that is poetry" (S, p. 109). This statement clearly wishes to redefine the modernist view of "nothing" as the void. What does it mean to "say" nothing? Or to "do" nothing: "The art of life, of a poet's life, is, not having anything to do, to do something" (J, April 29, 1852, p. 394). Having nothing to say and saying it, and doing something when having nothing to do—are these statements saying the same thing? Does it matter that the second statement was written in a journal by Henry David Thoreau in 1852, almost a century before Cage gave his "Lecture on Nothing"? I think it does, even though if one took a strictly historical context into account a different Thoreau might emerge. Nor is it in the spirit of Thoreau, whose overriding interest was in the "present moment," to suggest that historical context is solely of the essence when discussing influence in the making of art. In 1989, Cage began a text entitled "An Autobiographical Statement" as follows: "I once asked Arragon, the historian, how history was written. He said, 'You have to invent it.'"[28] In the history that Cage invented, Thoreau played no small part.

When Cage remarked in his "Lecture on Something" that "something and nothing are not opposed to each other but need each other to keep on going" (S, p. 129) he had yet to read Thoreau. But, when he read of doing something while "not having anything to do," as he did in the 1960s, one can begin to imagine his excitement, for he himself had written similarly: "Having nothing to do, we do it nonetheless."[29] Nineteenth-century antecedents to his independently discovered ultramodern views! Cage made that discovery, not through *Walden*, but in response to having heard the writer and naturalist Wendell Berry read aloud from the *Journal*.

It has been shown that *Walden* leads to, rather than departs from, the *Journal*. This diminishes the scholarly view of primacy, in either direction, and allows viewing them instead as complementary texts. However, that being said, there are still certain aspects of the *Journal* that understandably influenced Cage in a deeper way than had he read *Walden* first. For example, there is the distinction of closure. Unlike the open-endedness of Thoreau's *Journal* entries, *Walden* is tightly constructed according to the four seasons. In addition, as noted by Stanley Cavell, *Walden* structurally mirrors the *Bhagavad Gita:* both have eighteen parts (*SW*, pp. 117–118). As such, *Walden* is a traditionally constructed book, with very clear beginnings, middles, and ends. However, according to Cage, "Life is one. Without beginning, without middle, without ending" (*S*, "Lecture on Something," p. 134). For Cage, life and art were unopposed. And since musical discourse traditionally viewed art and life as decidedly separate (and still does for the most part), Cage attempted to move art into the direction of life: "Art's obscured the difference between art and life. Now let life obscure the difference between life and art."[30]

But, while shifting the focus from *Walden* to the *Journal*, it is important to note the similarities between Cage's move away from the human contrivance of art toward the direction of life uncontrived and Thoreau's shift of authorial emphasis in the *Journal* from a centered self in the direction of nature. That movement, leading the reader from the closed form of *Walden* to the open-ended form of the *Journal* by shifting the emphasis toward nature, is the same shift Cage intended by moving away from art and toward life.

In what follows, I will examine similarities between the writings of Cage and Thoreau's *Journal*. In particular, I will address the connection between Cage's and Thoreau's nondual approach to sound and silence and their resultant appreciation and acceptance of non-intention.

Cage believed that he shared Thoreau's views on sound and music. In 1958, he observed: "Where these ears are in connection with a mind that has nothing to do, that mind is free to enter into the act of listening, hearing each sound just as it is, not as a phenomenon more or less approximating a preconception" (*S*,

"Composition as Process," p. 23). If one subscribes to this aesthetic, many parallels between Cage and Thoreau can be found.

Cage saw his nineteenth-century predecessor as "a modern thinker."[31] What did Thoreau regard as "music"? On June 25, 1852, he wrote in his journal that "the music is not in the tune; it is in the sound" (*J*, p. 436). Charles Ives addresses this distinction in his *Essays before a Sonata:* "Thoreau was a great musician, not because he played the flute but because he did not have to go to Boston to hear 'the Symphony.'"[32] Kenneth W. Rhoads interprets the composer's statement as follows: "Ives was of course thinking of that same inner music which existed for Thoreau independent of concert halls, instruments, and performers."[33] Rhoads further explains that "on a somewhat more abstract level, he [Thoreau] perceived a music in the phenomena of nature."[34]

Cage would have considered Rhoads's analysis to be incorrect. So would Charles Ives, whose opinion is perhaps unintentionally refuted by Rhoads: "at this point arises one of those ostensible paradoxes which the student of Thoreau encounters frequently; for, despite his euphoric exaltation of music as man's supreme achievement, he not only knew very little about the art or its technical aspects but expressed an active antipathy for organized or formal music."[35] Ives considered Thoreau to be a "great musician." Rhoads seems to be saying that Thoreau, paradoxically, paid little attention to music.

The problem concerns how music is defined. Is Thoreau praising music in its formal setting? Hardly. He paid little attention to formal music, because that clearly was *not* what he meant by "music." F. O. Matthiessen illustrates this point, even though he also misunderstood it: "[H]is remarks about music all lead to this point. He is never really talking about the art of music, of which he knew next to nothing."[36] Cage, for his part, also expressed an antipathy to more formal kinds of musical activity. Long regarded as one of the most influential composers of this century, he professed to have little knowledge of what might be traditionally regarded as music's technical aspects. In an interview with William Duckworth, Cage offered these surprising remarks: "I don't have an ear for music, and I don't hear music in my mind before I write it. And I never have. I can't remember a melody . . . all those things which most musicians have, I don't have."[37]

Cage would say that Thoreau *is* talking about the "art of music" and it is precisely that which makes him a modern thinker. Thoreau's perceptions are descriptive, not abstract. "Reading the *Journal,* I had been struck by the twentieth-century way Thoreau listened. He listened, it seemed to me, just as composers using technology nowadays listen."[38] What the "experts" regard as traditional musical expression may, in fact, run counter to Thoreau's views on the appropriate nature of music. Perhaps this explains why some scholars consider his statements about music to be symbolic and abstract. But, for one of this century's greatest composers, Thoreau's ideas about music are not symbolic; instead, they define music's true and actual nature.

Emerson believed that the perceptions of a child were purer than those of an adult: "Most persons do not see the sun. At least they have a very superficial seeing. The sun illuminates only the eye of the man, but shines into the eye and the heart of the child."[39] On June 9, 1852, Thoreau extended that idea into the world of sound: "Ah, that I were so much a child that I could unfailingly draw music from a quart pot! Its little ears tingle with the melody. To it there is music in sound alone" (*J,* p. 421).

Cage long believed that all sounds were valid as music. In 1937, he predicted: "I believe that the use of noise to make music will continue and increase until we reach a music produced through the aid of electrical instruments which will make available for musical purposes any and all sounds that can be heard" (*S,* "The Future of Music: Credo," pp. 3–4). Noises were often part of Cage's sound palette, especially those not usually regarded as musical, "sounds like feedback, and fire or burglar alarms which we don't think of as music, the current musical underdogs."[40] What links Emerson and Thoreau's preference for a childlike perception to Cage's views regarding noise as music? Thoreau believed that what was noise for adults remained music to the ears of children: "children are fond of and make what grown people call a *noise,* because of the music which their young ears detect in it" (*J,* June 9, 1852, p. 422).

Cage composed music like what Thoreau himself heard by just listening. This is why Thoreau did not have to go to Boston to hear the symphony. For him, as with Cage, all sounds, all noises were music: "Nature makes no noise. The howling storm, the rustling leaf, the pattering rain are no disturbance, there is an essential and unexplored harmony in them" (*J*, November 18, 1837, p. 21).

When asked what he thought of as his most important legacy to future generations, Cage replied that it was "having shown the practicality of making works of art nonintentionally."[41] His compositions place sounds into the unintentional context of silence: "to me, the essential meaning of silence is the giving up of intention."[42] Thoreau regarded sounds in a remarkably similar way. "All sound is nearly akin to Silence; it is a bubble on her surface. . . . It is a faint utterance of Silence, and then only agreeable to our auditory nerves when it contrasts itself with the former. In proportion as it does this, and is a heightener and intensifier of the Silence, it is harmony and purest melody" (*J*, December 1838, p. 35). If there is an affinity between Cage and Thoreau regarding the nature of "silence," the key to discovering it lies in determining what role non-intention plays in their views on sound and music.

Cage believed that silence was the "giving up of intention." He also regarded the use of non-intention in artmaking as his greatest legacy. Can it be inferred that his music, being unintentional, produces a nondualistic equality between sound and silence? Perhaps the following remarks by Cage himself will provide an answer: "People often ask what music I prefer to hear. I enjoy the absence of music more than any other, or you could say silence. I enjoy whatever ambient sounds there are to hear."[43]

For Cage, there was no such thing as absolute silence. Silence is simply unintended sound. Those sounds constitute what Cage regarded as music. He used the example of his visit to an anechoic chamber, which was supposed to provide a silent environment: "I entered one at Harvard University several years ago and heard two sounds, one high and one low. When I described them to the engineer in charge, he informed me that the high one was my nervous system in operation, the low one my blood in circulation. Until I die there will be sounds. And they will continue following my death. One need not fear about the future of music" (S, "Experimental Music," p. 8).

A correlation between sound and music has already been demonstrated in the writings of Thoreau. The connection between sound and silence has also been established. How do Cage's views on non-intention relate to Thoreau's musical preferences?

The telegraph harp produced what Thoreau regarded as "the most glorious music I ever heard" (J, January 23, 1852, p. 329).[44] This "musical instrument" sheds some light on the relationship between his views on non-intention and music: "[I]t began to sound but at one spot only. It is very fitful, and only sounds when it is in the mood. You may go by twenty times, both when the wind is high and when it is low and let it blow which way it will, and yet hear no strain from it, but another time, at a particular spot, you may hear a strain rising and swelling on the string, which may at last ripen to something glorious" (J, January 21, 1853, p. 518). Thoreau cannot will the sounds of the telegraph harp. They independently exist. At some times the harp sounds; at other times it does not. Thus, the most glorious music Thoreau ever heard manifests itself non-intentionally.

Elsewhere, Thoreau is even more specific in proclaiming this music as unintentional. He suggests, as did Cage, that coincidence is usually preferable to a willed act: "Thus, as ever, the finest uses of things are the accidental. Mr. Morse did not invent this music" (J, January 23, 1852, p. 329). And if human invention is not the source of this music, what is? Clearly, it is nature itself. Thoreau's love of the telegraph harp indicates his preference for non-intentional sounds in the natural environment: "I can tell the extent to which a man has heard music by the faith he retains in the trivial and mean, even by the importance he attaches to what is called the actual world" (J, August 5, 1852, p. 470).

Cage shared Thoreau's affinity for the sounds of the natural world: "You know that I've written a piece called 4' 33", which has no sounds of my own making in it. . . . 4' 33" becomes in performance the sounds of the environment."[45] This composition requires no action; it simply indicates the passing of time. As one of his most famous works, it does for sound what Cage thought Robert Rauschenberg's *White Paintings* did to the visual image. It is a neutral surface, collecting the surrounding environment into the work itself.

4' 33" embodies what Cage and Thoreau regarded as music. The composer does not will any of the sounds.[46] Nor does the audience. Both ideally become observers of the environment. What Sharon Cameron considers relevant to Thoreau equally concerned John Cage: "Man is in the natural world as its witness or beholder, not as its explicator."[47] Such observation centers on what the poet Charles Olson regarded as "process not goal."[48] For Thoreau, this process was the effort, not the deed: "In a very wide but true sense, effort is the deed itself" (*J*, June 30, 1840, p. 57). Cage held a view similar to that of the Japanese potter Shoji Hamada: "I am not interested in the pot; I'm interested in the process of making it."[49]

By removing willful intent, observation becomes the logical extension of silence into the world of sound. And for Cage and Thoreau, observation is central to the role of the artist. The focus is on the observed, not the observer. On November 10, 1851, Thoreau wrote of "the so much grander significance of any fact . . . when not referred to man and his needs but viewed absolutely" (*J*, p. 300). Cage applied a similar method of "giving up your likes and dislikes and becoming interested in things. I think the Buddhists would say, 'As they are in and of themselves.'"[50] The role of the observer lies in following what Thoreau regarded as the highest form of communication, toward which he "can make no reply" and "lend only a silent ear" (*J*, September 14, 1841, p. 89). For Thoreau, "the highest condition of art is artlessness" (*J*, June 26, 1840, p. 56). To which Cage responds: "[T]he highest purpose is to have no purpose at all. This puts one in accord with nature in her manner of operation" (*S*, "45' for a Speaker," p. 155). Cage suggests that "I have nothing to say and I am saying it." Thoreau's reply: "Silence alone is worthy to be heard" (*J*, January 21, 1853, p. 518).

Silence and speech working together: such is the nondualistic nature of these terms for both Thoreau and Cage. As Norman O. Brown has observed, "Instead of symbolism—in a Symbol there is concealment and yet revelation: here therefore, by Silence and by Speech acting together, comes a double significance—instead of words of silent power, the impossibility of language."[51] This directly opposes the symbolic view Sherman Paul professes: "For sound and silence were Thoreau's grand analogy: silence was a celestial sea of eternity, the general, spiritual and immutable; sound was the particular and momentary bubble on its surface."[52] And it is Thoreau himself who offered the best defense for a nonsymbolic interpretation: "Why give each other a sign to keep? If we gave the thing itself, there would be no need of a sign" (J, February 7, 1841, p. 69). This passage refutes the idea of correspondence and, written in 1841, it does so early on.

Not surprisingly, it is *Walden* that writers like Paul regard as primary, a stance that colors their interpretation of Thoreau's other work. *Walden* is clearly a symbolic text.[53] As Sherman Paul remarks, "In *Walden*, at once his victorious hymn to Nature, to her perpetual forces of life, inspiration and renewal, Thoreau defended his vocation by creating its eternal symbol."[54]

Walden was written for a public that saw "a ground for complaint if a man's writings admit of more than one interpretation" (W, "Conclusion," pp. 289–290). Thoreau was writing to his "neighbors": "I do not propose to write an ode to dejection, but to brag as lustily as chanticleer in the morning, standing on his roost, if only to wake my neighbors up" (W, "Where I Lived and What I Lived For," p. 76). For John Cage, as I have noted, Thoreau's message to that public was directed through the question: "Is life worth living? *Walden* is his detailed and affirmative reply."[55]

If *Walden* says yes, the *Journal* offers no such response. This text is rooted in questions. In his review essay devoted to Sharon Cameron's *Writing Nature*, David S. Gross comments that "[w]hat Cameron sees in the 'Thoreau' of the *Journal* is a man for whom all questions of meaning—especially analogical meanings in the relations of man and nature—come increasingly to *remain* questions."[56] This method of observation, which poses questions yet seeks no answers, is similar to Thoreau's distinction between looking and seeing: "I must let my senses wander as my thoughts, my eyes see without looking" (*J*, September 13, 1852, p. 488). For Thoreau, seeing was distinguished from looking by removing the intermediary of intellect: "I begin to see such objects only when I leave off understanding them" (*J*, February 14, 1851, p. 184).

Thoreau sought experience (seeing), not understanding (looking). His preference for sensual experience rather than intellectual insight is what separates the *Journal* from *Walden*. Thoreau used symbols as insightful answers, thus *Walden*'s goal as a symbolic text. But Thoreau's journals document his life, a process of posing questions. Such unanswered questions are the result of unmediated observation. Philip F. Gura believes that the study of language "returned him to the things of this world, not to a shadow universe of transcendental forms."[57] Thus, the practice of his profession led Thoreau to the observation of life as art. The "impossibility of language" that Norman O. Brown suggests caused a move away from the symbolism of language toward a description of the thing itself.[58]

Many scholars have been confounded by Thoreau's "ostensible paradoxes."[59] Such confusion has led to opposing views of his writings. Why, for example, would someone who apparently preferred experiential observation use language that communicates in symbols? Why would an author who Joel Porte believes wished to live the "purely sensuous life,"[60] write the following in his *Journal:* "Certainly the heart is only for rare occasions; the intellect affords the most unfailing entertainment" (*J*, December 31, 1851, p. 316).

This debate among Thoreau scholars has been oppositional because it is dualistically constructed. Cage regarded this as "dualistic thinking which opposes for example the Apollonian to the Dionysian."[61] For him, "the separation of mind and ear had spoiled the sounds" (*S*, "Lecture on Nothing," p. 116). Thoreau also removed such separations: "All beauty, all music, all delight springs from apparent dualism but real unity" (*J*, March 20, 1842, p. 103). Thoreau's "apparent dualism" has confounded the critics. It is "real unity"—the removal of separations between sound and silence, art and life, sense and intellect—that reveals his nondualistic thinking.

To better comprehend the "both/and" perspective of Cage and Thoreau, one must be acquainted with the nondualistic thinking that informs the Asian philosophies that so strongly influenced both men.[62] From 1960 to 1961, John Cage was a fellow at Wesleyan University's Center for Advanced Studies. While there, he was asked to compile a list of the ten books that had most influenced his views. Several have roots in Indian and Chinese philosophical thought. The list includes *The Transformation of Nature in Art*, by Ananda K. Coomaraswamy, and the *Doctrine of Universal Mind* of Huang Po.[63] Thoreau, too, was influenced by Indian and Chinese philosophy. As Arthur Christy has said, "one could go through Thoreau's *Journal*, culling passage after passage to illustrate his fondness for Oriental books."[64]

There is an emphasis on process and nondualistic thinking in Asian aesthetic thought. Seasons are an important natural process that both Thoreau and Cage used in their work. Cage, in an early composition called *The Seasons*, "looks to their symbolic meaning as interpreted through Indian philosophy: spring as regeneration, summer as preservation, fall as destruction, and winter as quiescence."[65] The obvious parallel is Thoreau's construction of *Walden* according to the four seasons. Moreover, the book shares the formal structure of the *Bhagavad Gita*. And as Arthur Christy has noted, "no one Oriental volume that ever came to Concord was more influential than the *Bhagavadgita*."[66]

Indian aesthetics thus played an important role in the work of both Thoreau and Cage. As the latter has remarked, "I was very impressed . . . years and years ago, by the reason for making art given by Ananda K. Coomaraswamy in his book, *The Transformation of Nature in Art*, in which he said that the business of the artist's responsibility is to imitate nature in her manner of operation."[67] Thoreau would have seen music as fulfilling Coomaraswamy's belief that art must imitate natural processes: "Music is the sound of the circulation in nature's veins" (*J*, April 24, 1841, p. 81).

It was Zen Buddhism, however, that John Cage regarded as having had the most influence on him. He recalled, for example, that "Daisetz Suzuki often pointed out that Zen's nondualism arose in China as a result of problems encountered in translating India's Buddhist texts."[68] The Zen master Huang Po has said: "[A]s soon as thought or sensation arises, you fall into dualism. Beginningless time and the present moment are the same. There is no this and no that."[69] According to Arthur Versluis, "Thoreau did not know of Zen Buddhism."[70] However, as Arthur Christy discovered, "Thoreau translated and edited portions of the Buddhist scriptures under the title of 'The Preaching of the Buddha.'"[71] The translation was from French into English. The French language does not specifically distinguish between "here" and "there." The French equivalents, "voici" and "voilà," have essentially interchangeable meanings. Thus, perhaps Thoreau became aware of nondualism in the same fashion as did the Chinese: through the problems of translation.

John Cage had a well-documented affinity for mystics, from Meister Eckhart to Norman O. Brown. It is not surprising that many critics view Thoreau in this light, with Cavell explicating the "open acknowledgment of his mysticism" (*SW*, p. 9), and Christy proclaiming that "his place is with the mystics."[72] Ananda K. Coomaraswamy describes an artistic genre that aptly characterizes the aesthetic to which Cage and Thoreau subscribed: "Another kind of art, sometimes called romantic or idealistic, but better described as imagist or mystical, where denotation and connotation cannot be divided, is typically developed throughout Asia in the second millennium. In this kind of art no distinction is felt between what a thing 'is' and what it 'signifies.'"[73]

For Cage and Thoreau, there was no separation between music and sounds, sounds and silence. Nor was there a distinction between symbol (what is "signified") and the thing itself (what "is"). Thus, the question of dualism, either in the direction of the self or of nature, is at the heart of what separates scholars when interpreting Thoreau. The discovery that nondualism is central to such interpretation ultimately connects opposing views. It explains the remarkable affinity between Henry David Thoreau and John Cage. It also clearly outlines the distinction between the aesthetics of Emerson and Ives and the aesthetics of Thoreau and Cage.

PART TWO/POETRY AND MUSIC

All deep things are Song. It seems somehow the very central essence of us, Song; . . . The Greeks fabled of Sphere-Harmonies: it was the feeling they had of the inner structure of Nature; that the soul of all her voices and utterances was perfect music. Poetry, therefore, we will call musical Thought. The Poet is he who thinks in that manner. . . . See deep enough, and you see musically; the heart of Nature being everywhere music, if you can only reach it.

—Thomas Carlyle ("The Hero as Poet")

THE TRANSPARENT EYE/I

Positioning the Self in Pound-Tradition Poetics

I become a transparent eyeball; I am nothing; I see all; the
currents of the Universal Being circulate through me; I am
part or parcel of God.

—Ralph Waldo Emerson (*Nature*)

The peculiarity of a work of genius is the absence of the
speaker from his speech. He is but the medium.

—Henry David Thoreau (*Journal*, January 27, 1852)

The Emersonian "eye": such transparency remains within the
concrete "I" of the self. Thoreau's use of the self attempted to
make the "I" transparent. Rather than becoming an emanating
source of vision, this self simply observes phenomena. These
disparate positions inform two kinds of contemporary poetry,
projective and objective verse.

The active "eye" is a projective "I," and lies at the heart of
the Emersonian aesthetic Charles Olson presented in his essay
"Human Universe": "END, which is never more than this instant,

than you on this instant, than you, figuring it out, and acting, so. If there is any absolute, it is never more than this one, this instant, in action."[1] On the other hand, there is the objective "I," which observes rather than projects. Thoreau's method of observation required a transparency of the self, not projected into space, but as an objective witness: "I hear and forget to answer. I am occupied with hearing."[2] Compare this to William Carlos Williams: "What do I do? I listen, to the water falling. . . . This is my entire occupation."[3] Nancy Willard regards such listening as an attempt to make the self invisible, allowing the thing to be, in and of itself. The poet must not only "free his work from ideas that did not come from the things themselves; he must free it from all traces of his own personality."[4]

This chapter will address distinctions between the Emersonian "eye" and the invisible "I" Willard discusses. I will begin with a look at "process" and how various poets interpret this idea. Process is a common link between projective and objective aesthetic views. Comparing them will show two distinct methods in using process as a source for artistic expression.

John Cage has said that he "couldn't stomach Emerson."[5] On the other hand, Thoreau's writings, in addition to Asian philosophy, are recognized as one of the two "most important influences on Cage's music."[6] I will contend here that the reason for such a dichotomy between Emerson and Thoreau is the same reason that separates the poets discussed. The primacy of process is a shared concern. However, the mechanism is drastically different. What is the position of the self in the writings of these poets? Is it the "transparent eye" of Emerson, or the "transparent I" of Thoreau?

PROCESS AS PRECURSOR

The function of art at the present time is . . . to draw us
nearer to the process which is the world we live in.
—John Cage (*For the Birds*)

For John Cage, the process of making has long been the source of his artistic creations. While Cage's methodology has always been controversial in musical circles, process has a long tradition in the making of poetry. Robert Creeley believes that process as a poetic source dates back to Whitman: "Not only does Whitman anticipate the American affection for the pragmatic, but he equally emphasizes that it is space and process which are unremittingly our condition."[7] Poets under the influence of Pound all agree on the importance of process. Cage devoted an entire lecture to the subject of composition as process.[8] Charles Olson may have written the most famous words on the subject: "The motive, then, of reality, is process not goal."[9] And finally, Louis Zukofsky posits the idea in the world of poetry: "A poem. This object in process—."[10]

There is also consensus on the unfinished nature of the work of art, both in the beginnings of this century and now. In 1926, Gertrude Stein said that "there is singularly nothing that makes a difference a difference in beginning and in the middle and in ending. . . ."[11] The same idea can be found in the writings of John Cage: "The early works have beginnings, middles, and endings. The later ones do not. They begin anywhere, last any length of time."[12] This aesthetic perception has both scientific and philosophical roots.

Two major scientific discoveries led to a drastic shift from the created object as a goal to the process of making as an end in itself. I will discuss one later. The other is the early work of Einstein, which single-handedly dismantled the Newtonian conception of the world. After Einstein, the universe was no longer a mechanized creation permanently and unchangeably designed. It was no longer possible for science to be able eventually to explain its nature. The goal of "understanding" was thus beyond the reach of mortal humanity, as was the Enlightenment's dream of the rationally directed perfecting of humankind. There were—and it could be scientifically proved—"no beginnings, middles, or ends." The universe, according to Einstein, is constantly in flux. Our world is a world of relativity. Thus, the twentieth century marks an end to the possibility of science as an absolutist religion. However, it also marks the flowering of a philosophy built upon such uncertainty: existentialism.

The philosopher William Barrett believes that both existen-

tialism and modern art stem from the central crisis of the twentieth century: the dismantling of rationalism as part of the foundation of Western civilization. Of existentialism and its relation
to this century's artistic practices, Barrett comments: "The more
closely we examine the two together, the stronger becomes the
impression that existential philosophy is the authentic intellectual expression of our time, as modern art is the expression of
the time in terms of image and intuition."[13]

However, according to Barrett, there are two views about
the actual nature of existential philosophy, those typified by Jean-
Paul Sartre and Martin Heidegger. Sartre believes that humanity
expresses itself in action, with our existence defined solely *by*
action. Heidegger posits "being" as prior to existence: "For without the open clearing of Being into which man can transcend
himself, he could not ex-sist, i.e., stand out beyond himself."[14]

Barrett believes that Heidegger is the true existentialist. He
views Sartre as a "Cartesian rationalist,"[15] for whom the duality
of mind and body continues to exist. For Sartre, existence is determined solely by one's actions. If actions are intellectually
willed, then existence determined by actions remains an existence in which intellect is primary: "In Sartre what becomes primary is . . . the will to action."[16]

If, on the other hand, Heidegger is the "true existentialist,"
this places his use of phenomenology, developed by his teacher
Edmund Husserl, within the context of existentialism. Phenomenology, for Heidegger, is "the attempt to let the thing speak
for itself." Barrett further explains that "according to Heidegger
we do not know the object by conquering and subduing it but
rather by letting it be what it is and, in letting it be, allowing it
to reveal itself as what it is."[17] It is in this sense that Heidegger
retains a phenomenological view of the "thing-in-itself."

These two philosophical stances mirror the Olson/Wil-
liams poetic axis: Olson's "man in action" is closely related to
Sartre's, while Williams's "no ideas but in things"[18] is expressed
philosophically by Heidegger. Olson viewed humanity as a projection into space, conflicting rather than coexisting with nature. Nature is "other," and as Olson said about Melville (and by

inference America as well), it is "the will to overwhelm nature that lies at the bottom of us as individuals and a people." [19] In contrast, Charles Tomlinson remarks that "Williams marks an historic moment for modern poetry in that his work sees the disappearance of all dualism." [20] In a nondualistic universe there can be no "other."

Although these poets, and those who might be grouped with them, agree on the primacy of process, they do not agree upon the nature of its implementation. There are two distinct methods of process at play in such poetic work. One centers upon the self projected into space (nature); the other emphasizes observing and describing the space itself, with humanity simply one coexistent aspect of it. For Charles Olson and the projectivists, the poetic process concerns the projection of humanity *into* nature, a dualistic view. For William Carlos Williams and the objectivists, process concerns observing humanity and nature collectively in a nondualistic manner.

Both of these processes are possible within the context of another major scientific discovery, Werner Heisenberg's "principle of 'indeterminism.'" Buckminster Fuller puts it concisely: "the act of measuring always alters that which is being measured." [21] For Olson, the response to Heisenberg was that since one cannot observe without changing the thing being observed, description is not accurately possible. Thus, "art does not seek to describe but to enact." [22] For artists who do not view nature and humanity as dualistically separate, however, description *is* possible. Such poets are aware of a continually shifting reality, a truly indeterminate process where changes occur outside the projection of human control. This vision proposes individual consciousness as simply one aspect of a larger existence. In that context, description becomes an expression of existence that, although including individual perception, is not exclusively mediated by it. George Oppen offered such a description in his poem "Route":

> . . . One man could not understand me because I was saying
> simple things; it seemed to him that nothing was being
> said. I was saying: there is a mountain, there is a lake. [23]

William Carlos Williams has remarked, "I cannot say more than how."[24] Marjorie Perloff concurs: "The *how*, for Poundians, thus becomes more interesting than the *what*: if poetry teaches us how to talk to ourselves, it is not because it provides us with a vision of Reality but because its processes imitate the processes of the external world as we have come to know it."[25] This accurately describes the process used by those poets regarded in this chapter as objectivists. But, for the poets who follow Olson, Pound does not represent process as that of the external world. It is instead the process of humanity *in* the world. Albert Gelpi's position concerning Pound best describes the relation to the projectivists: "Whereas Marjorie Perloff would emphasize the collage-like character of *The Cantos* and argue that the discontinuity between the bits and fragments produces indeterminacy of meaning, I emphasize the intentional continuity between bits and fragments to create a meaningful gestalt."[26] It is not, in other words, the perception of the material that creates a poetic discourse; it is the interaction between the individual and the material.

These views seem, at first glance, incongruous. Yet both are equally present in the poetry of Ezra Pound. This is best expressed in the first part of the definition of "imagism," a poetic movement he helped to found: "Direct treatment of the 'thing,' whether subjective or objective."[27] Even though imagism was short-lived, its allowing for the coexistence of objective and subjective poetic stances keeps it highly influential as a method of making poetry. According to Hyatt Waggoner, "The best known Imagist poem, kept alive by anthologists and literary historians chiefly to illustrate what Imagist poems ought to be like, is Pound's 'In a Station of the Metro.'"[28] This two-line poem reads:

The apparition of these faces in the crowd;
Petals on a wet, black bough.[29]

"Direct treatment of the 'thing'" seems to imply a nonsymbolic presentation of material and, as such, to separate Pound from the Emersonian tradition. But symbolism is only one manifestation of the real difference being addressed in this analysis: the role of the creative self in the making of art.

Is "The apparition of these faces in the crowd" an objectively direct treatment of the thing? "Faces in the crowd" is a simple enough observation, but the word "apparition" is problematic. Is it an "unusual or unexpected" sight or a "ghost"-like figure? The first definition remains capable of being objective, but the second, which most of us know as the usual sense of the word, is suspect. Read singly, this line could be seen as either objective or subjective; and, after all, either reading falls within Pound's definition.

The second line, "Petals on a wet, black bough," is more easily aligned with an objective treatment of the thing. But, what about the possibility of connection *between* the lines? Are the "faces in the crowd" being described as "petals on a wet, black bough"? Is the poet taking a subjective stance toward the work by playing with an analogous relationship? Or are the lines merely two separate experiences that coexist in parallel? Both approaches are possible. And, in fact, these approaches inform the direction of either projective or objective verse.

A comparison of two critical views of Pound's *Cantos*, Perloff's collage-like discontinuity versus Gelpi's thesis of poetic continuity, mirror respectively the objective and subjective poles of Pound's definition of imagism. Such a comparison also shows a remarkable closeness to M. H. Abrams's metaphors of "mirror and lamp." Abrams places them historically as follows: "The first of these [mirror] was characteristic of much of the thinking from Plato to the eighteenth century; the second [lamp] typifies the prevailing romantic conception of the poetic mind."[30] Olson's individual in action is a lamp that projects light (the individual) into space. Oppen's description of things is, on the other hand, a mirror that simply seeks to observe a phenomenon as it is. However, while Abrams describes a mirroring that represents *objects* in nature (an admittedly outdated mode of artistic expression), Oppen's mirror represents the *process* of nature. This is a radical departure from both the classical tradition and its romantic continuation.

Thus, even though Pound is the source for both of these poetic directions, two completely different interpretations of his work follow from that influence and inform the direction of two separate poetic discourses.[31] At the heart of such difference is the relation between humanity and nature. One assumes a dualistic separation from nature requiring the illumination of humanity into space. The other, nondualistic view mirrors the process of nature as an inclusive entity, of which humanity is an integral part. I will now address both views individually.

PROJECTIVE VERSE: THE TRANSPARENT EYE

It is Emerson who best anticipates the projectivists. Robert Creeley has said that his famous remark "form is never more than an extension of content" originates with Emerson's sense of how poetry takes place: "in his [Emerson's] sense of *spontaneous form*. I was thinking of Waggoner's insistence that all American verse is from Emerson's,[32] not tutelage but from Emerson's perception of its nature."[33] Emerson believed in the "lordship over nature" that Charles Olson saw as the aim of Americans:[34] "Nature is thoroughly mediate. It is made to serve. It receives the dominion of man as meekly as the ass on which the Saviour rode."[35] Early in his writing career, Emerson viewed the human relationship to nature as separate ("Philosophically considered, the universe is composed of Nature and the Soul")[36] and heroic ("One after another his victorious thought comes up with and reduces all things, until the world becomes at last only a realized will,— the double of the man").[37]

Olson believed Melville's *Moby-Dick* to be a precursor to projective verse. However, a careful look at both Melville's work and *Call Me Ishmael*, Olson's interpretation of the romance, reveals great disparities. For Melville, Ahab's heroic attempt at "lordship over nature" ends in tragedy. "Call me Ishmael," the narrator insists at the beginning of *Moby-Dick*, and it is he, the witness, who survives. Unlike Ishmael, Charles Olson's heroic stance projects the human will into space. He is no witness. Olson begins *Call Me Ishmael* with this statement: "I take SPACE to be the central fact to man born in America."[38] To which Paul Christensen adds, "Olson is urgent on this point—the whale is the 'SPACE' which he says it is the character of the American to wish to subdue."[39] In Olson's interpretation of *Moby-Dick*, Ahab's battle with the whale is a battle between humanity and space. In other words, nature and humanity are in conflict. Olson's Ahab is a heroic figure who attempts to harness nature through the force of human will. "The last of the heroes," his "primordial passions are beyond blame. . . . It is merely a fact of being human."[40] Olson is inappropriately described by Christensen's subtitle, *Call Him Ishmael.* One should instead call him Ahab.

Olson completely misinterpreted Melville: "It is space, and its feeding on man, that is the essence of his [Melville's] vision, . . . it is time which is at the heart of Christianity."[41] For Olson, time and space were opposed. Earlier in the book, however, he expressed a markedly different view: "Melville had a way of reaching back through time until he got history pushed back so far he turned time into space."[42] Melville would, I suspect, completely agree. *Moby-Dick* chronicles the reconciliation of humanity and nature and critiques the dualistic position Olson sees as central to the text. Ahab is not a sympathetically heroic character. He is, instead, the embodiment of a romantic nature Melville saw as doomed to destruction.[43]

Reason and the primacy of human intellect are ultimately destroyed by the "inscrutable" white whale. The whale is not a simplistic characterization of space. It carries the deeper meaning of all that cannot be understood, of an unknown that refuses to be harnessed. Whereas Olson believed that "the Pacific is the end of the UNKNOWN,"[44] Melville believed there was no end to the unknown. The whale wins the battle—and after defeating Ahab, still inscrutable, it completely disappears.

For Melville, the attempt to control nature led to complete and utter destruction, which only Ishmael survives. In a final contrast to Olson's analysis, note that the piece of flotsam which saves him, a coffin, was fashioned by the ship's carpenter. Salvation by the work of a carpenter sounds decidedly like a Christian ending to a text Olson perceived as having been written "for no holy purpose."[45]

Olson saw process as "the most interesting fact of fact (the overwhelming one, how it works, not what, in that what is always different if the thing or person or event under review is a live one, and is different because adverbially it is changing)."[46] One assumes from this that all of nature is in the constant process of change. And in his most famous essay, "Projective Verse," Olson's "Objectism" seems to be proclaiming an affinity with the objectivists: "Objectism is the getting rid of the lyrical interference of the individual as ego, of the 'subject' and his soul, that peculiar presumption by which western man has interposed himself between what he is as a creature of nature . . . and those other creations of nature which we may, with no derogation, call objects. For a man is himself an object, whatever he may take to be his advantages."[47] This statement seems to place humanity and nature in the same plane of existence. Has Ahab been transformed into Ishmael?

Contrast "Projective Verse" with the opening lines of "The Kingfishers": "What does not change / is the will to change."[48] This shows the distinction Olson made between humanity and nature. As George Butterick explains, "It is not change itself that is unchanging, the fact of it, but man's will."[49] The human "will to change" does not change. Thus, although nature is perceived as being in flux, human beings carry within them the possibility of at least this one absolute. The assertion of the human will in the midst of change is reminiscent of Sartre's position that existence is determined solely by action. And, as previously noted, that affinity results in a dualistic relationship between nature and humankind.

Edward Dorn sees Olson's *Maximus Poems* as positing humanity "distinct from nature."[50] For Dorn, Olson's construction of Gloucester as a place is only interesting as it relates to the person of Maximus. Nature is only valuable as it relates to humankind: "Because place, as a non human reality, is simply outside the presentments of human meaning. And not interesting."[51] Dorn considers being abstract "one of the lovely qualities of Western Man. . . . What I mean by abstract is, as far purely away from nature as he can get, thus bringing into fruition all the properties of man, simply."[52] With characteristic frankness, Dorn remarks that "there is nothing I detest so much as objectivity."[53] So much for humans as objects!

There is an underlying separation between nature and the self among projectivist poets. Not all such poets are as adamant as Dorn, and even his position was less strident by the time he wrote *Gunslinger*. However, the common source of that separation is their position on the importance of relationship in poetic discourse.[54]

For Olson, "It comes to this: the use of a man, by himself and thus by others, lies in how he conceives his relation to nature."[55] He appreciates the objective clarity of the "thing." However, what is central is its relationship to the self: "the thing itself, and its *relevance* to ourselves who are the experience of it."[56]

In Edward Dorn's *Gunslinger*, the narrative "I" disappears from the poem, only to return as Parmenides' secretary. According to Michael Davidson, Parmenides believed that "self and other are one and the same—that in order for one to conceive of sensible objects at all he must be *part* of those objects as well."[57] If the "I" is now in the service of a nondualistic philosopher, then perhaps Dorn has changed his views on the separation between nature and the self. And, in fact, one learns from Dorn that Heidegger's "mind is equal to the poem [*Gunslinger*]."[58] Does this signal a nondualistic shift in the poetry of Edward Dorn? Not necessarily. He is still in the process of making connections, trying to "make things cohere. I make structures and edifices, more like bridges."[59] Thus, even though Marjorie Perloff believes that Dorn's epic, *Gunslinger*, is "perhaps best understood as a poetic Sourcebook on postmodern discourses,"[60] syntactically the poet is still in the driver's seat. Dorn, not the reader, is making connections between the text and its meaning. As the "Horse" exclaims in *Gunslinger*,

What makes Process and Reality heavy
   is the &![61]

Robert Creeley had a long association with Charles Olson. According to Paul Christensen, "Creeley remains a tireless apologist for Olson's work and the ideas that sustained the group of poets who initially formed around him."[62] Creeley, however, seems to hold affinities that conflict with Olson's aesthetic views. The most obvious example is Creeley's appreciation of John Cage. Martin Duberman states that Olson and the "painter crowd" at Black Mountain College tended to view Cage and his "crowd" as "somewhat precious and self-indulgent."[63] In 1952 Olson wrote "A Toss, for John Cage," which is critical of Cage's use of chance operations:

> about vessel, ask this old dog to ask his 64 numbers,
> the 16 trigrams, a question, have him throw his 3 pennies
> (the old Three, dat old number) to find you out in what way
>   his 20 Minutes
> despite all the new wine therein (I'll believe his discoveries)
> is not a bottle, is
> so blown, doth
> intervene, hath
> beginning. And ends
> like an hexameter.[64]

Creeley, on the other hand, mentions Cage as a source of inspiration. When asked by Ekbert Faas if there is "any modern music which you feel moves in directions you follow in your poetry," Creeley responds, "Well, sure, Cage is fascinating to me, for example."[65]

But Creeley's work, in ways that I will describe below, differs markedly from that of Cage. Cage would have agreed with his view on the relation between body and mind: "I think that if we want a center for experience now, it is this sense, that the mind and body are one."[66] However, Cage would have further insisted that the work be non-intentional, removing self-expression as a part of artistic discourse. Cage used the following anecdote to explain his position: "I wrote a sad piece and people hearing it laughed. It was clearly pointless to continue in that way, so I determined to stop writing music until I found a better reason than 'self-expression' for doing it."[67]

As Ron Silliman points out, it is impossible to remove the intent of the poet when the writing is centered on the projective sense of breath: "the off-balance, breath-imitating line of the Black Mountain poets, especially Robert Creeley and the early Charles Olson, foregrounds the presence of a speaker by setting up a physiological distinction between that persona and the internal rhythms of the reader." Later, Silliman concludes that these kinds of poems' "fundamental commitment at the level of the reader's experience is to passivity, to the subject which can only observe, incapable of action."[68] The writer's intentions are thus embedded in the breath of the line itself.[69]

Another important distinction between Cage and Creeley (and, by association, all projectivist poets) turns on the issue of relationships in the writing of poetry. Cage wished to let "sounds be sounds" and wanted his audience to stop "responding in terms of relationships of sounds."[70] Creeley, on the other hand, considers the issue of relationships central to his poetic views. In his novel *The Island,* he comments: "it is only in the relationships men manage, that they live at all."[71] For Robert Creeley, all things relate in some sense. No one is an "island."

Robert Duncan's poetry affirms Creeley's point of view. In "The Law I Love Is Major Mover," Duncan writes:

> Look!   the Angel that made a man of Jacob
>   made Israël in His embrace
> was the Law,   was Syntax.
>   Him I love is major mover.[72]

Thus Duncan, through syntax, also has an affinity for the connections, bridges, and relationships found in the writings of the poets under consideration. His work contains other elements that have been characterized as "projective":

Often I am permitted to return to a meadow
as if it were a given property of the mind
that certain bounds hold against chaos,

that is a place of first permission,
everlasting omen of what is.[73]

This "given property of the mind" assumes a capability of control. Duncan, in setting the intellect apart from its surroundings, allows for the possibility of refuge within the self. Thus the intellect is capable of separation from "chaos," setting forth a dualistic position between humanity and the environment.

Lee Bartlett is correct in his assessment of Robert Duncan's sensibility as a poet: "Duncan's version of the world, version of art, is romantic, as the poet emerges not as a giver of meanings but as a revealer of them."[74] Such revelation is part and parcel of M. H. Abrams's "lamp" metaphor. As for the mirror, and the ability to reflect reality, Robert Creeley examined that in *The Island.* Mirrors break: "What had broken was only a mirror, and a very unreal one, but it was all they saw themselves in. They had made it, both of them, with what care they possessed."[75]

For the projectivists, reality is a construct always in danger of disintegrating. Nature, in constant flux, cannot be trusted. The reality of an individual consciousness is only tested when it is projected into a "field" of action. Nature and the self coexist, but with Emerson's qualification: "nature is the opposite of the soul, answering to it part for part."[76]

Emerson said that "man is an analogist, and studies relations in all objects."[77] This statement is but one example of the link between Emerson and projective verse.[78] Surprisingly, the projectivists have, on this point, found an ally in Melville; in this regard, as Paul Christensen sees it (and I agree), Olson's analysis is correct: "his [Melville's] vision at the end of the novel, according to Olson, is of a world of relatedness."[79] In *Moby-Dick,* Melville affirms this analysis: "there is no quality in this world that is not what it is merely by contrast. Nothing exists in itself."[80]

But Melville has an ally that the projectivists do not: nature. For as Ishmael represents the integration of nature with the self, so Melville critiques the separation that informs the Emersonian roots of projective verse.

In an interview with Ekbert Faas, Robert Duncan exclaims, "I read Modernism as Romanticism; and I finally begin to feel myself pretty much a 19th century mind."[81] In the matter of the self as a poetic identity, the same might be said for the projectivists as a whole.

OBJECTIVE VERSE: THE TRANSPARENT "I"

This chapter has shown that Emerson is a primary source for projectivist thought. For the objectivists, Thoreau is the source. In 1851, he wrote of "the so much grander significance of any fact—of sun and moon and stars—when not referred to man and his needs but viewed absolutely!"[82] Thoreau was interested in the actual perception of things, not in their relation to the perceiver. So are the objectivists.[83]

The "subject" in objective verse is the individual self. And although the self is present in the work for the objectivist, the individual poet does not attempt to mediate the poetic experience. Instead, as George Oppen has written, the poet's self is situated "among things."[84] Thus, in an "objective" view the poet coexists *within* what is perceived. The subject is distinguished from the object only when viewed subjectively. Subjectivity presupposes a mediating self. For the objectivists, one does not "relate" to the object, nor can the subject be distinguished entirely from the object. Nature is not a separate entity, and reality is not mediated solely by the self. In a nondualistic universe, there are no absolutes. The objective self is a de-centered self, where even the "will to change" is subject to change.

The self is not separate from nature in objective poetry. In *Paterson*, William Carlos Williams exclaims,

> Be reconciled, poet, with your world, it is
> the only truth![85]

Williams believed that this holistic view of artists and their world could only exist through reconciliation.

> Divorce is
> the sign of knowledge in our time,
> divorce! divorce! [86]

The position of humanity distinct from nature was "the sign of knowledge in our time." The projectivist is "divorced" from nature. Objectivists move in opposition to that knowledge. For them, the self is *of* the world, there is no separation. These poets sought to create a world in which humanity coexists rather than controls.

Williams suggested that the separation of humanity from nature is the status quo of knowledge "in our time." Thus, it is not surprising that George Oppen viewed Charles Olson, whose projective verse regards humanity and nature separately, as "simply not an encounter with a new poetry." [87] Although Rachel Blau DuPlessis uses Oppen's statement as a means of connecting Olson with Pound, there is another, more pertinent reason for Oppen's view: the position of self in relation to the world. He does not directly attack Olson on this point, but his poetry indirectly does:

> The power of the mind, the
> Power and weight
> Of the mind which
> Is not enough, it is nothing
> And does nothing
>
> Against the natural world,
> Behemoth, white whale, beast
> They will say and less than beast,
> The fatal rock
> Which is the world— [88]

Human conflict with nature produces the tragedy Melville illustrated in *Moby-Dick*. Against nature, humanity cannot compete.

The white whale, that "fatal rock" of nature, signals the failure of human efforts to control the natural world. Oppen chooses to coexist within nature, describing the natural world as if it were the human world as well. Unlike Olson, whose self-based poetic repeats the tragic vision of Ahab, Oppen mirrors the experience of the white whale (nature) that Melville believed was beyond human understanding:

'Substance itself which is the subject of all our planning'
And by this we are carried into the incalculable. [89]

Melville himself described the white whale as unpaintable.[90] For Oppen, reconciliation with the world carried one into the incalculable. The result was a movement away from the possibility of human understanding and control, leaning toward unmediated experience of and coexistence with nature. Thoreau himself perhaps described this objectivist position best: "I begin to see such objects only when I leave off understanding them."[91] Objectivists wish to coexist, to live experientially in harmony with their environment. In Zukofsky's "A"-12, as Barry Ahearn explains, it is "not that a conflict exists between mind and the elements; when the relations between mind and the world are properly seen, they are discovered to be harmonious."[92]

How is nature experienced in poetic form? William Carlos Williams believed that in poetry "you do not *copy* nature, you make something which is an *imitation* of nature."[93] This once again suggests the "mirror" of M. H. Abrams. For Williams, the imitation of nature is "perhaps a transit from adjective (the ideal 'copy') to verb (showing process)."[94] John Cage also regarded art forms as imitations of nature, mirroring Williams's description of the movement away from representation and toward process: "the responsibility of the artist is to imitate nature in its manner of operation."[95] How does nature operate? For Williams, "there is only, we might say, flux in nature."[96] Thus the process of nature is a process of constant change.

The study of substance leads to the incalculable, and the process of making poetry is a process of change. As Marjorie

Perloff has written of Gertrude Stein: "Substances are defined by what they are not, but what they *are* remains open to question. And Gertrude Stein wants it that way because her real subject is change."[97] The subject of change is the experience of the natural world. And in the world of things, where understanding is no longer a goal, the process of experience is the only possibility. Such perception exists beyond human understanding. It is an acceptance of the innate mystery of the world. According to Nancy Willard: "[A]ll things flower under the hand of the man who asks nothing but to know them as they know themselves. Things are immeasurable, ungraspable, and mysterious."[98]

No objectivist could have written "The Kingfishers." The opening line "what does not change," is antithetical to objective verse. *Everything* changes. In his or her own way, each objectivist poet seeks the experience of Jackson MacLow: "We wanted to be able to allow the 'world' . . . to express itself in our works, rather than merely our personal egos."[99]

The "will to change," Olson's symbol of constancy, is remarkably absent from objective poetry. These poets attempted to express the world without active mediation of the human will. To express the "thing itself," the ego must remove any desire to control. For William Carlos Williams, poetry was the "thing itself": "That thing, the vividness which is poetry by itself, makes the poem. There is no need to explain or compare. Make it and it *is* a poem. This is modern, not the saga. There are no sagas— only trees now, animals, engines: There's that."[100] Once again, Thoreau is a precursor to such thinking, as Joel Porte suggests: "Thoreau was determined to stick with the thing-in-itself."[101] Objectivists do not willfully project themselves into the environment. They simply observe.

Michael Heller regards "An Objective" by Louis Zukofsky as "one of the major statements of a 'poetics' of the twentieth century, a document which now looms as nearly equal in force to Pound's Imagist manifestos or Charles Olson's 'Projective Verse.'"[102] The comparison to Olson is particularly appropriate to my analysis, since Zukofsky's text is remarkably at odds with Olson's. For Zukofsky, "Shapes suggest themselves, and the mind senses and receives awareness."[103] Rather than "enact," as Olson prescribed in "Projective Verse," Zukofsky's poetry is "a kind of attentive readiness."[104] Olson's *Maximus* is a heroic epic, whereas Zukofsky's *"A,"* also sometimes described as an epic, omits the hero. This marks an important distinction between projective and objective verse. As Charles Bernstein has noted, Olson's "heroic stance translates into a will to dominate language rather than let it be."[105] In contrast, Zukofsky's *"A"* is "less concerned with the actions of some hero than with the possibilities of attention."[106]

In "Human Universe," Charles Olson posits the human condition as "you on this instant . . . in action."[107] For Williams, "the perfect type of the man of action is the suicide."[108] Thus, for objectivists, the sole appropriate "act" is the removal of self. Williams, in agreement with the words from Thoreau that began this chapter, also saw the poet as a medium: "Why even speak of 'I,' he dreams, which / interests me almost not at all?"[109] Williams lets the poetic perception speak without any mediation of self. The result is a transparent "I," whose sole purpose is to remove intent and let the object simply "be." This is the meaning behind Williams's "no ideas but in things,"[110] and, as Marjorie Perloff discovers, it is closely related to a sentiment shared by John Cage: "Not ideas but facts."[111]

The objectivist poet observes the "thing itself," becoming the "witness" George Oppen describes:

Because the known and the unknown
Touch,

One witnesses—.[112]

As these poets witness phenomena, the will subsides and observation begins. Such de-centered observation is a courageous act: "The act of courage—which is another way of talking about the issues Oppen has been dealing with—is an act in which self is put out of consideration."[113]

Objectivists affect such detachment in a variety of ways.

John Cage and Jackson MacLow use a method called "chance operations," where the artist consults a system outside the self when making creative decisions.[114] Cage also shared, with Pound and Zukofsky, an affinity for collage. This method obscures the self by applying a multiplicity of intentions to the work, what Marjorie Perloff regards as the "radical decentering characteristic of Poundian collage."[115] Gertrude Stein wrote in *Tender Buttons*, "Act so that there is no use in a centre."[116] *Tender Buttons* is an excellent example of such de-centered writing. In it, Stein removed the connections of syntax, a technique William Carlos Williams greatly admired: "Stein has gone systematically to work smashing every connotation that words have ever had, in order to get them back clean."[117]

All of these methods attempt to detach the self as a connecting force between the poem and its reader. In objectivist poetry, relationships, which are so central to Creeley, along with the corresponding "bridges" and syntax of Dorn and Duncan, have been removed. Meaning is no longer centered in the poet. Nor does the poet provide the connections that help determine meaning. As Ron Silliman suggests, the meaning of the writing can only be constructed "through its actual elements *combined with* experiences of the reader. It is, as Jackson MacLow argues, 'perceiver centered.'"[118]

The reader builds the bridges, forms the syntactic connections, and determines their relationship to the text. As Barry Ahearn observes: "By refusing to be the god of his poem, Zukofsky invites participation by the reader . . . the poem becomes a process to be completed, not a code to be deciphered."[119] Charles Bernstein confirms the distinction between this approach and that of the projectivists, in this case Charles Olson: "unlike the imaginative collaboration required by a Stein or Zukofsky, many of Olson's poems need a *scholarly* collaboration to make them intelligible."[120]

Objective poetry is the expression of what Thoreau regarded as "silence": "To the highest communication I can make no reply; I lend only a silent ear."[121] For John Cage, "the essential meaning of silence is the giving up of intention."[122] Cage and Thoreau thus consider removal of the willful self as both the true meaning of silence and the highest of artistic expressions.

This silent self is a recurrent theme among objectivist poets, manifested in their view of the world. The unmediated observation of nature requires a silence of the self. As William Carlos Williams has explained, when "of earth his ears are full, there is no sound."[123] Men and women experience silence in their perceptions of nature. For George Oppen, the world is "the great mineral silence," a "process/Completing itself."[124]

In his poem "Route," Oppen described his motivations for making poetry:

> Clarity, clarity, surely clarity is the most beautiful
>   thing in the world,
> A limited, limiting clarity
>
> I have not and never did have any motive of poetry
> But to achieve clarity[125]

In "Of Being Numerous," Oppen defined his experience of what clarity signifies for him:

> Clarity
>
> In the sense of *transparence,*
> I don't mean that much can be explained.
>
> Clarity in the sense of silence.[126]

"Clarity in the sense of silence"; the world in process *as* silence; the removal of self *in* silence: an observation that is experienced rather than understood. This is not just the motive of Oppen's poetry but that of all objective verse. His "sense of transparency" manifests itself as a "transparent I."

Objectivist poetry is the experience of textual silence. In *Tender Buttons,* Gertrude Stein suggests that such silences need not be expressed as absence. They may instead be approached as John Cage approached them: by a coexistent self created by asking questions. As Janice Doane comments: "In the 'Rooms' section of *Tender Buttons* the issue of silence is raised in the form of questions: 'Why is there that sensible silence. . . . Does silence choke speech or does it not.'"[127] And Henry David Thoreau wrote in his *Journal* that "[t]he longest silence is the most pertinent question most pertinently put. Emphatically silent. The most important question, whose answers concern us more than any, are never put in any other way."[128] Tellingly, regarding Stein's questions, Doane continues, "These questions are not answered."[129]

Once again, as in Chapter 2, questions remain questions. And yet, the decision to let them remain as such is still a decision—a decision to remove the controlling self: "The conclusion came when there was no arrangement. All the time that there was a question there was a decision."[130] The decision of not answering allows for the self to coexist rather than control; a "silence which is there is not disturbed by expression."[131] In "Rooms" Gertrude Stein is pushing at boundaries, playing against them by asking questions, and the issue of silence predominates. In "What Happened," she writes: "silence is so windowful."[132] According to Doane, "Besides the pun on wonderful, 'windowful' also suggests a room full of windows, of many different perspectives, or, more ironically, that Stein felt she was achieving, for all her 'muddy prose,' a certain *clarity* and even *transparency*."[133] Such clarity, mirroring that of George Oppen, produces a method of writing that eschews symbolic references: "The stamp that is not only torn but also fitting is not any symbol. It suggests nothing."[134] To "suggest nothing" is best evoked by William Carlos Williams's poem "To Have Done Nothing," which reads in its entirety:

No that is not it
nothing that I have done
nothing
I have done

is made up of
nothing
and the diphthong

ae

together with
the first person
singular
indicative

of the auxiliary
verb
to have

everything
I have done
is the same

if to do
is capable
of an
infinity of
combinations

involving the
moral
physical
and religious

codes

for everything
and nothing
are synonymous
when

energy *in vacuo*
has the power
of confusion

which only to
have done nothing
can make
perfect [135]

This is what John Cage addressed in his "Lecture on Nothing": "I have nothing to say and I am saying it and that is poetry." [136] Such poetry finds aesthetic roots in the writings of Thoreau: "The art of life, of a poet's life, is, not having anything to do, to do something." [137] For Thoreau, and the objectivists as well, "silence alone is worthy to be heard." [138]

SILENCING THE SOUNDED SELF

The Poetry and Music of John Cage

What we require is silence;
but what silence requires is that I go on talking.

—John Cage ("Lecture on Nothing")

In this chapter I will address John Cage's inclusive desire to allow room for silence in both his musical compositions and written texts. Cage himself noted that "silence" had been a lifelong concern:

> I've lately been thinking again about *Silence,* which is
> the title of my first book of my own writings. When I was
> twelve years old I wrote that oration that won a high school

oratorical contest in Southern California. It was called "Other People Think," and it was about our relation to the Latin American countries. What I proposed was silence on the part of the United States, in order that we could hear what other people think, and that they don't think the way we do, particularly about us. But could you say then that, as a twelve year old, that I was prepared to devote my life to silence, and to chance operations? It's hard to say.[1]

Proving a lifelong devotion to chance operations, Cage's method of achieving silence, would be difficult. However, his entire body of work has, from the very beginning, been devoted to the inclusion of silence in an otherwise sound-filled world.

One of the first ways in which Cage allowed silence into music was, in sharp contrast to Ives, by emphasizing duration instead of harmony. In the 1930s Cage studied with the Austro-Hungarian composer Arnold Schoenberg, who emigrated to the United States in 1933 and eventually settled in Los Angeles. Regarding his work then, Cage recalled:

> After I had been studying with him for two years, Schoenberg said, "In order to write music, you must have a feeling for harmony." I explained to him that I had no feeling for harmony. He then said that I would always encounter an obstacle, that it would be as though I came to a wall through which I could not pass. I said, "In that case I will devote my life to beating my head against that wall."[2]

Cage found two allies in his battle with harmony: the French composer Erik Satie and Anton Webern, a former student of Schoenberg's.[3] In a lecture given at Black Mountain College in 1948, Cage remarked:

> In the field of structure, the field of the definition of parts and their relation to a whole, there has been only one new idea since Beethoven. And that new idea can be perceived in the work of Anton Webern and Erik Satie. With Beethoven

the parts of a composition were defined by means of harmony. With Satie and Webern they are defined by means of time lengths. The question of structure is so basic, and it is so important to be in agreement about it, that one must now ask: Was Beethoven right or are Webern and Satie right?

I answer immediately and unequivocally, Beethoven was in error, and his influence, which has been as extensive as it is lamentable, has been deadening to the art of music.[4]

For Cage, duration became a means of getting around the difficulty of having "no feeling for harmony." And by citing Webern, Cage was able to use one of Schoenberg's most famous pupils as an example of how harmony was an erroneous method of structuring music.

It was silence that pointed Cage away from harmony and toward duration. As he saw it, harmony as a structuring method does not include silence:

If you consider that sound is characterized by its pitch, its loudness, its timbre, and its duration, and that silence, which is the opposite and, therefore, the necessary partner of sound, is characterized only by its duration, you will be drawn to the conclusion that of the four characteristics of the material of music, duration, that is, time length, is the most fundamental. Silence cannot be heard in terms of pitch or harmony: It is heard in terms of time length.[5]

At this point, one could very well question Cage's logic. If duration, by nature, includes silence, while harmony, in and of itself, does not, does it follow that duration is the only possible approach to structuring music? Obviously not. However, this view does shed light on Cage's underlying motivation in believing that such was the case. Harmony requires the imposition of unity upon musical material. It is a humanly contrived method of writing music that cannot be directly found in nature. Although C-major chords may be naturally derived, their structural relationships, as found in so-called tonal music, obey a carefully (and humanly) constructed system of rules. Cage, on the other hand, was looking for justification outside any musical tradition. He was attempting to uncover a structural connection between the making of music and the natural world. His effort had little to do with how music is conceived; it was instead an attempt to uncover how music is perceived. In other words, Cage was paying more attention to how we actually hear music than he was to how we think about music.

When we consider how music is heard, unrelated to how it is made (if that is possible), then, indeed, duration is more fundamental than harmony. We hear sound and silence, and we can do so directly with neither thought nor preconception.[6] To hear harmony, as a preconceived structure of relationships between tones, requires a process that includes a knowledge of certain musical procedures and traditions that have as much to do with thinking as they do with hearing.

In 1948, when he wrote his "Defense of Satie," Cage still saw composition as a unifier of experience: "an activity integrating the opposites, the rational and the irrational" (S, "Composition as Process," p. 18). And, in another text, Cage extends such abstractions into concrete musical terms: "The material of music is sound and silence. Integrating these is composing" (S, "Forerunners of Modern Music," p. 62). However, by looking toward natural rather than human designs, he was already on a path away from such ordered procedures: "there is a tendency in my composition means away from ideas of order towards no ideas of order" (S, "Composition as Process," p. 20). In 1958, he delivered a lecture at Darmstadt, Germany, entitled "Composition as Process," from which the preceding quotation is drawn. The first part of this lecture discusses changes in his approach to composition. These changes describe a process of moving away from "ideas of order," not away from order itself. The question continually raised in Cage's work is *whose* order will determine the course of the art experience. And the issue of duration involves a first step away from human derivation and human control.

From the 1930s onward, Cage used what is known as square root form, one of his first attempts at structuring music by duration rather than by pitch. Macrostructure and microstructure coincide, so that if there are four measures per unit there will be four units; if the internal phrasing of the bars is 1-2-1, the external division of parts (within the large structure of four units) will also be 1-2-1. For example, in his *First Construction in Metal* (1939), there are sixteen measures in each structural unit. To make the square root, there are, consequently, sixteen units. The large structure is divided symmetrically as follows: four, three, two, three, four, thus totaling sixteen, and each individual unit is similarly divided. This method, used in Cage's music during the 1930s and 1940s, eventually produces a formal structure independent of its content. Content, in this period, was still primarily a matter of taste, as can be seen, for example, in Cage's selection of piano preparations for his *Sonatas and Interludes:* "The materials, the piano preparations, were chosen as one chooses shells while walking along a beach. The form was as natural as my taste permitted" (*S*, "Composition as Process," p. 19). On the other hand, Cage observed of the form of the *Sonatas:* "nothing about the structure was determined by the materials which were to occur in it; it was conceived, in fact, so that it could be as well expressed by the absence of these materials as by their presence" (*S*, "Composition as Process," pp. 19–20).[7]

Interchangeability of content in a fixed structure is equally apparent in his "Lecture on Nothing" (ca. 1950), written soon after he created *Sonatas and Interludes* (1946–1948). This lecture is an early example of how Cage took structural ideas from music and used them in creating texts. And it is this approach that characterizes a continuing relationship between Cage's music and text through the mid-1970s (at which point this study ends): "In writing my 'literary' texts, I essentially make use of the same composing means as in my music."[8]

The "Lecture on Nothing" uses square root form and is described as such by Cage, in a way characteristic of many of his later texts, through an introduction to the published lecture: "There are four measures in each line and twelve lines in each unit of the rhythmic structure. There are forty-eight such units, each having forty-eight measures. The whole is divided into five large parts, in the proportion 7, 6, 14, 14, 7. The forty-eight measures of each unit are likewise so divided" (S, p. 109). Thus, one is informed of exactly how Cage made the structure. In this case, an integrating of rational and irrational would see structure (form) as rational and content as irrational, or what Cage then regarded as the integration of mind and heart (S, "Composition as Process," p. 18).

As a formal invention, Cage's use of square root form does suggest the direction of music first, text second. However, in keeping with my initial thesis that music and text interact, Cage's "Lecture on Nothing" contains certain important ideas not previously discernible in his musical work. First and foremost is the distinction between the "integration of opposites" and having "nothing to say" and "saying it" (S, p. 109). What still applies as a formal idea no longer holds as content. Cage's writing is non-intentional, whereas integration, still present in the relation between form and content, demands a very specific intention. Thus, although Cage's innovations regarding compositional form move from music to text, certain innovative ideas move from text to music.

The most important of those ideas is the coexistent nature of sound and silence, of something and nothing: "I have nothing to say and I am saying it and that is poetry as I need it" (S, p. 109). This remark, cited in brief above, is from the beginning of Cage's "Lecture on Nothing." Its origin in his aesthetic is twofold. First, Cage's attempts at art as communication were, according to him, miserable failures. A prepared-piano piece, The Perilous Night (1943–1944), is one example. Based on "an Irish folktale he remembered from a volume of myths collected by Joseph Campbell," The Perilous Night concerns "a perilous bed which rested on a floor of polished jasper. The music tells the story of the dangers of the erotic life."[9] After a critic wrote that the last movement sounded like "a woodpecker in a church belfry," Cage responded: "I had poured a great deal of emotion into the piece, and obviously I wasn't communicating this at all. Or else, I thought, if I were communicating, then all artists must be speaking a different language, and thus speaking only for them-selves. The whole musical situation struck me more and more as a Tower of Babel."[10] Cage decided, from that point on, to stop composing music until he found a reason other than communi-cation for writing it.

Second, "having nothing to say" provided the rationale that allowed Cage to continue composing. It was through Gita Sarab-hai, an Indian musician who was studying Western music with Cage, that he learned "the traditional reason for making a piece of music in India: 'to quiet the mind thus making it susceptible to divine influences.'" According to Cage, this led music away from self-expression and toward self-alteration through the in-fluence of the natural environment: "We learned from Oriental thought that those divine influences are, in fact, the environ-ment in which we are. A sober and quiet mind is one in which the ego does not obstruct the fluency of the things that come in through our senses and up through our dreams."[11]

"Having nothing to say" allows that environment the op-portunity to speak. In Cage's work, partially as a result of his studies of Asian religion and philosophy beginning in the 1940s, it is a process of diminishing the role of the self in the creative act. He was especially influenced in this regard by reading Al-dous Huxley's anthology *The Perennial Philosophy*.[12] This book describes a religious mysticism found in both East and West:

> The divine Ground of all existence is a spiritual Absolute, ineffable in terms of discursive thought, but (in certain cir-cumstances) susceptible of being directly experienced and realized by the human being. This Absolute is the God-without-form of Hindu and Christian mystical phraseology. The last end of man, the ultimate reason for human exis-tence, is unitive knowledge of the divine Ground—the knowledge that can come only to those who are prepared to "die to self" and so make room, as it were, for God.[13]

Cage, more often than not, tried to emphasize the removal of separations between West and East. Consequently, it was of great significance when, after Cage learned the Indian reason for making music, his friend the composer Lou Harrison, while "reading in an old English text, I think as old as the sixteenth century, . . . found this reason given for writing a piece of music: 'to quiet the mind thus making it susceptible to divine influences.'"[14] This approach to composition was no longer linked to one culture; it was universal in the original sense of the word.[15] Found in all cultures, such quietude was a reaching out into the world around us, a removal of the separation between self and world—a nondual view of reality.

Thus, although Cage's "Lecture on Nothing" is compositionally dual, in that form and content still combine the rational and the irrational, the written content is nondual: "I have nothing to say *and I am saying it.*" "What silence requires is *that I go on talking.*" Such statements are obviously paradoxical and thus plainly influenced by Cage's study of Zen. In his introduction to *The Zen Teaching of Huang Po,* John Blofeld, the translator, comments: "At first sight Zen works must seem so paradoxical as to bewilder the reader. On one page we are told that everything is indivisibly one Mind, on another that the moon is very much a moon and a tree indubitably a tree."[16] And even though silence as a phenomenon outside the self had entered into several of Cage's musical compositions, both in the 1930s and 1940s, his "Lecture on Nothing" is the first instance in which silence is produced through such paradox: within the self, via what Cage considered his most important legacy, "[h]aving shown the practicality of making works of art nonintentionally" (*CC,* p. 25 [1985]).

Non-intention had become, for Cage, a new, nondualistic realization of what silence really was. His visit to an anechoic chamber had proved to him that, in the dualistic sense of sound versus silence, there "was no silence." There were only intended and unintended sounds.

Cage's first recorded instance of unintended sound was textual: "I have nothing to say and I am saying it." This goes an important step beyond just having nothing to say. It implies what Cage makes specific in his "Lecture on Something" (ca. 1951): "This is a talk about something and naturally also a talk about nothing. About how something and nothing are not opposed to each other but need each other to keep on going" (*S*, p. 129). And although Cage does not make non-intentional texts formally until long after having accomplished this in musical compositions, he does manage to address the idea of non-intentional content in a text before he is able to do so in music.

It is through chance operations that Cage begins making unintentional music. For him, it was an extremely unorthodox way of Zen practice:

> [R]ather than taking the path that is prescribed in the formal practice of Zen Buddhism itself, namely, sitting cross-legged and breathing and such things, I decided that my proper discipline was the one to which I was already committed, namely, the making of music. And that I would do it with a means that was as strict as sitting cross-legged, namely, the use of chance operations, and the shifting of my responsibility from the making of choices to that of asking questions. (*CC*, pp. 42–43 [1979])

Although persons conversant with Zen might not view Cage's practice as Buddhism, it did serve as a very effective method of composing.

Beginning around 1950, Cage began to use the *I Ching* (Book of Changes) as a source of response to his compositional questions.[17] In his foreword to Richard Wilhelm's German translation, C. G. Jung writes:

> The axioms of causality are being shaken to their foundations: we know now that what we term natural laws are merely statistical truths and thus must necessarily allow for exceptions. We have not sufficiently taken into account as yet that we need the laboratory with its incisive restrictions in order to demonstrate the invariable validity of natural law. If we leave things to nature, we see a very different picture: every process is partially or totally interfered with by chance, so much so that under natural circumstances a

course of events absolutely conforming to specific laws is almost an exception.

The Chinese mind, as I see it at work in the *I Ching*, seems to be exclusively preoccupied with the chance aspect of events.[18]

Although Jung used the *I Ching* as a means of discovering the unconscious mind within, Cage saw it as a way of getting outside the mind altogether; a way of allowing nature, the environment, or what Zen would call Mind with a capital *M* to respond to his compositional questions.

As Cage frequently mentioned, he had conceived the idea of a "silent piece" earlier than 1952, when *4'33"* received its premiere. The notion was first publicly mentioned in an address entitled "A Composer's Confessions" given on February 28, 1948, before the National Inter-Collegiate Arts Conference at Vassar College:

> I have, for instance, several new desires (two may seem absurd but I am serious about them): first, to compose a piece of uninterrupted silence and sell it to Muzak Co. It will be 3 or 4½ minutes long—those being the standard lengths of "canned" music—and its title will be *Silent Prayer*. It will open with a single idea which I will attempt to make as seductive as the color and shape and fragrance of a flower. The ending will approach imperceptibility.[19]

This "single idea" became a process of making music that Cage learned from Ananda K. Coomaraswamy: "I have for many years accepted, and I still do, the doctrine about Art, occidental and oriental, set forth by Ananda K. Coomaraswamy in his book *The Transformation of Nature in Art*, that the function of Art is to imitate Nature in her manner of operation."[20] Cage used the *I Ching* as a way of "imitating nature in her manner of operation," and by constructing his *4'33"* through chance operations he did indeed find a method of making a process parallel to the seductiveness of "the color and shape and fragrance of a flower." It was

Cage's use of chance operations that made possible a formal design to place the silence in. And when one listens to the silence of *4'33"*, one hears nature.

However, following nature in her manner of operation proved to be problematic. Cage realized that, even though *4'33"* was made solely of non-intended sounds, he was still providing the frame. Even if, as was the case with that piece, the length of the frame was chosen non-intentionally through chance operations, Cage was still making a fixed object.

This eventually ran counter to his notion that things "become" in processes rather than as fixed objects: "You say: the real, the world as it is. But it is not, it becomes! It moves, it changes! It doesn't wait for us to change. . . . It is more mobile than you can imagine. You are getting closer to this reality when you say as it 'presents itself'; that means that it is not there, existing as an object. The world, the real is not an object. It is a process."[21]

Nor does the "silent piece" sufficiently address Cage's professed nondualism, where "something and nothing" are unopposed—*4'33"* allows the unintentional into music. The performer simply sits and listens as the audience listens. As such, this piece exemplifies a movement toward the silence of "nothing" and the acceptance of non-intentional sounds. But what about intentional sounds? Are these accepted? At what point in *4'33"* does Cage allow the performer (or the composer, for that matter) to produce the "something" of intentional sounds? How can something and nothing be unopposed if only "nothing" is allowed? These are, of course, rhetorical questions, and as such their answers are obvious. Something and nothing can be unopposed only if both intention and non-intention equally coexist.

These questions sent Cage in the direction of indeterminacy, and in 1958 he began his series of *Variations*.

> The first one was involved with the parameters of sound, the transparencies overlaid, and each performer making measurements that would locate sounds in space. Then, while I was at Wesleyan [University], in this first piece I had

had five lines on a single transparent sheet, though I had had no intention of putting them the way I did, I just drew them quickly. At Wesleyan while talking to some students it suddenly occurred to me that there would be much more freedom if I put only a single line or a single notation on a single sheet. So I did that with *Variations II* but it still involved measurement. (*CC*, p. 110 [1965])

Next followed a piece without measurement entitled *Variations III*, written between December 1962 and January 1963. Richard Kostelanetz implies that it solves some inherent problems with the published version of *4'33"*, among them, of course, the measurement of time:

> Since Cage invariably takes the intellectual leaps his radical ideas imply, he subsequently concluded that not only were any and all sounds "music," but the time-space frame of *4'33"* was needlessly arbitrary, for unintentional music is indeed with us—available to the ear that wishes to perceive it—in all spaces and at all times. (*Variations III* [1964], he once told me over dinner, is so open, "We could be performing it right now, if we decided to do so.")[22]

The published score includes a title page with the statement: "*Variations III* for one or any number of people performing any actions." There are no prescribed genres, either in music or any other medium, except that the piece is to be "performed." Nor are the actions themselves determined, except for the possibility that there will be actions. The instruction page then reads:

> Two transparent sheets of plastic, one having forty-two undifferentiated circles, the other blank. Cut the sheet having circles in such a way that there are forty-two small sheets, each having a complete circle. Let these fall on a sheet of paper, 8½ × 11. If a circle does not overlap at least one other circle, remove it. Remove also any smaller groups

of circles that are separated from the largest group, so that a single maze of circles remains, no one of them isolated from at least one other. Place the blank transparent sheet over this complex.

Starting with any circle, observe the number of circles which overlap it. Make an action or actions having the corresponding number of interpenetrating variables (1 + n). This done, move on to any one of the overlapping circles, again observing the number of interpenetrations, performing a suitable action or actions, and so on.

Some or all of one's obligation may be performed through ambient circumstances (environmental changes) by simply noticing or responding to them.

Though no means are given for the measure[me]nt of time or space (beginning, ending or questions of continuity) or the specific interpretation of circles, such measurement and determination means are not necessarily excluded from the "interpenetrating variables."

Some factors though not all of a given interpenetration or succession of several may be planned in advance. But leave room for the use of unfor[e]seen eventualities.

Any other activities are going on at the same time.[23]

As the following brief analysis will show, in this piece Cage created a truly nondual composition that allows both something and nothing to coexist equally.

Cage's use of transparencies is one of the best methods he ever devised to ensure an indeterminate composition. The usual score, even one where chance procedures determine it, is fixed. Once printed, the notation, by nature, is unchanged. This produces an object, and Cage fully realized that. Such is the case even with his *Music for Piano* series, for example, where the notations are merely his observations of imperfections in the score paper, and in the elaborately constructed series of chance operations used to make *Williams Mix:* "All the cutting, all the splicing of the *Williams Mix* is carefully controlled by chance operations. This was characteristic of an old period, before indeterminacy in performance, you see; for all I was doing then was renouncing my intention. Although my choices were controlled by chance operations, I was still making an object."[24]

Through transparencies, however, the score need not be initially fixed. For example, in *Variations III* one drops circles on a page, which results in a collection of interpenetrating circles. However, there are multiple possibilities as to how many circles remain, if they intersect, and how many must be removed if they do not. The composer certainly does not determine that; nor does the performer. Even though the score is eventually fixed, it can be fixed differently for each performance. Furthermore, if there is more than one performer, there can also be more than one determined score. While fixity still exists in Cage's transparency scores, the variables are so numerous (hence the title "variations") that it would be next to impossible to determine what exactly will be fixed and what will remain open.

If the score itself seems variably determined, the performer's interaction with it is even more variable. By looking at a circle, one simply observes how many interpenetrations there are between it and any other connecting circle and then performs an action for each observed interpenetration. Such actions can be either planned or unplanned, although Cage does insist that room be left to do both. Observing "ambient circumstances" can either lead to an action or can actually *be* the action. Because there is no indicated time measurement and because "other activities are going on at the same time," once begun, a performance of *Variations III* need never end. One could follow the score for a time, enter into the experience of an ambient circumstance, and continue reacting to that and other circumstances indefinitely. Or, as Cage noted:

Just as I came to see that there was no such thing as silence, and so wrote the silent piece, I was now coming to the realization that there was no such thing as nonactivity. In other words the sand in which the stones in a Japanese garden lie is also something. . . . And so I made *Variations III*, which leaves no space between one thing and the next and posits that we are constantly active, that these actions can be of any kind, and all I ask the performer to do is to be aware as much as he can of how many actions he is performing. I ask him, in other words, to count. That's all I ask him to do. I ask him even to count passive actions, such as noticing that there is a noise in the environment. We move through our activity without any space between one action and the next, and with many overlapping actions. The thing I don't like about *Variations III* is that it requires counting, and I'm now trying to get rid of that. But I thought that performance was simply getting up and then doing it. (*CC*, pp. 110–111 [1965])

On the other hand, one need not count past an environmental experience if one chooses to remain in it. And Cage himself understood the difficulties: "But what (how and why) are we counting? Since there are no gaps between one action and another (and many of them overlap) do we know when something is finished and the next begins? The situation is irrational."[25] In fact, it is the openness of *Variations III*, where the rational and the irrational coexist without reconciliation, that allows the performer to enter into or go out of the piece at will, all the while paradoxically staying within its notated structure. Thus, intention and non-intention equally coexist, even as, because of the several layers of experiences going on at the same time, a multiplicity of intentions collectively produce an unintentional and indeterminate piece. In *Variations III* something and nothing really do need each other; they coexist in a fabric of art and life completely interwoven one with another. Cage once spoke of a conversation with the visual artist Willem de Kooning: "I was with de Kooning once in a restaurant and he said, 'If I put a frame around these bread crumbs, that isn't art.' And what I'm saying is that it is. He was saying it wasn't because he connects art with his activity—he connects with himself as an artist whereas I would want art to slip out of us into the world in which we live" (*CC*, pp. 211–212 [1978]). In *4'33"* Cage placed a frame around the "bread crumbs," thus beginning the process of dismantling dualistic separations such as the one mentioned between art and life. In *Variations III*, nondual experience is complete: the final impediment, the frame, is removed.

If, as I have suggested here, the lectures on both "nothing" and "something" inform the musical directions Cage pursues in *4'33"* and *Variations III*, it is equally true that those two compositions point toward his future developments in literature. The gestation period was long. In 1968, Richard Kostelanetz remarked of Cage's second book: "What is most conspicuously lacking in *A Year from Monday* is an analogous path-breaking gesture that could command as much suggestive influence for literature as his earlier 'musical' demonstrations."[26] This, in and of itself, need not matter. Many composers have also been writers, and there is usually no consequent claim asserted that somehow the writing must be up to the same level as the music. Frequently, and this is as true of Cage as of many others, the writings are an explanation of what is happening in the music, as I pointed out in the discussion of Ives. Thus it is not a common expectation that a composer's writings must somehow qualify as literature.

However, Cage implies from the very first that, in some cases at least, his writings go beyond musical explanation. As Cage observed in his foreword to *Silence:*

> When M. C. Richards asked me why I didn't one day give a conventional informative lecture, adding that that would be the most shocking thing I could do, I said, "I don't give these lectures to surprise people, but out of a need for poetry." . . .

As I see it, poetry is not prose simply because poetry is in one way or another formalized. It is not poetry by reason of its content or ambiguity but by reason of its allowing musical elements (time, sound) to be introduced into the world of words. (*S*, p. x)[27]

It is in this context then, that one might expect a literary critic (which is the hat Kostelanetz most frequently wears) familiar with Cage's musical inventions to express disappointment in the less revolutionary nature of his texts.

Cage's writing in the 1960s had more to do with his developing sensibilities as a poet than it did with trying to equal his achievements in music. On the other hand, two textual inventions are worthy of note: his mesostics and his diaries, only one of which (the diaries) is germane to this analysis.[28]

Cage used the diary form for many years, beginning in 1965 and ending with his eighth diary in 1982. His "Diary: Audience 1966," while not a part of the "Diary" series, is short and has the same formal structure as his other diaries. I received permission from Cage to use photocopies of pages from the stenographic notepad that he employed in composing this piece. These were obtained from the John Cage papers at the Wesleyan University Archives, and they serve as the raw material for this analysis. Although Cage did not leave detailed information about how those materials were used, he did leave a trail, in various sources, through which I will try to reconstruct the compositional process.

The first place to check for clues is the introduction to the text, where Cage frequently provided information about how his pieces were written:

This text was written on the highways while driving from an audience in Rochester, New York, to one in Philadelphia, Pennsylvania. Following the writing plan I had used for *Diary: Emma Lake*, I formulated in my mind while driving a statement having a given number of words. When it had jelled and I could repeat it, I drew up somewhere along the road, wrote it down, and then drove on. When I arrived in Philadelphia, the text was finished.[29]

The full title of the source Cage mentions is "Diary: Emma Lake Music Workshop 1965." This introduction reads:

> Just before setting out for Saskatchewan to conduct a music workshop at Emma Lake in July 1965, I received a request from the editor of *Canadian Art* for an article having fifteen hundred words. Since I was busy with a number of projects, I was on the point of replying that I had no time, when I noticed that I would be at the workshop for fifteen days and that if I wrote one hundred words a day it wouldn't be too much for me and the magazine would get what it wanted. . . .
> Instead of different type faces, I used parentheses and italics to distinguish one statement from another. I set the text in a single block like a paragraph of prose. Otherwise I used the mosaic-discipline of writing described in the note preceding *Diary: How to Improve* etc. *1965.*[30]

The "Diary" introduction just mentioned reads: "It is a mosaic of ideas, statements, words, and stories. It is also a diary. For each day, I determined by chance operations how many parts of the mosaic I would write and how many words there would be in each. The number of words per day was to equal, or, by the last statement written, to exceed one hundred words."[31]

With the information provided by these introductions, analysis can begin. The first page of Cage's notebook (Figure 1) includes the working title "On Audience" and shows a series of numbers to the left of the roman numerals I–VI. These roman numerals correspond to the six large sections of the text. As I will demonstrate, everything but the six is explainable according to the procedures previously described. However, one thing that characterizes all of Cage's work is that every compositional decision had a reason behind it, even if the decision was not to de-

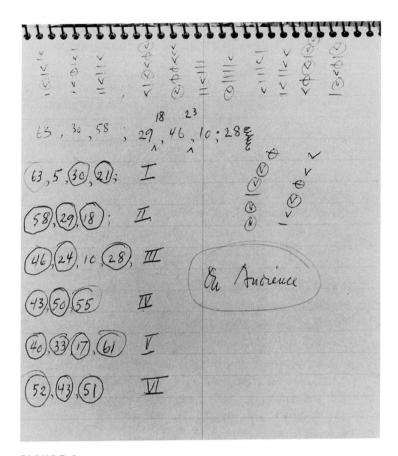

FIGURE 1.

cide. Why six? Two clues offer a plausible answer. First, Cage claims to have followed the same procedure in writing "Audience" that he used for "Emma Lake." That diary had fifteen parts, one for each day of the workshop. In Cage's introduction to "Audience" he writes that it was composed while driving from Rochester to Philadelphia. And—not coincidentally I believe—in 1965 the approximate driving time for this trip was six hours.[32] Thus, the large structure may have been conceived by writing at a hundred words per hour!

The first page also has thirteen hexagrams derived from the *I Ching*, with some (but not all) of the corresponding numbers written out below. Cage discussed how he employed the *I Ching* in "To Describe the Process of Composition Used in *Music of Changes* and *Imaginary Landscape No. 4*":

> What brings about this unpredictability is the use of the method established in the *I Ching* (*Book of Changes*) for the obtaining of oracles, that of tossing three coins six times.
>
> Three coins tossed once yield four lines: three heads, broken with a circle; two tails and a head, straight; two heads and a tail, broken; three tails, straight with a circle. Three coins tossed thrice yield eight trigrams (written from the base up): *chien*, three straight; *chen*, straight, broken, broken; *kan*, broken, straight, broken; *ken*, broken, broken, straight; *kun*, three broken; *sun*, broken, straight, straight; *li*, straight, broken, straight; *tui*, straight, straight, broken. Three coins tossed six times yield sixty-four hexagrams (two trigrams, the second written above the first) read in reference to a chart of the numbers 1 to 64 in a traditional arrangement having eight divisions horizontally corresponding to the eight lower trigrams and eight divisions vertically corresponding to the eight upper trigrams. A hexagram having lines with circles is read twice, first as written, then as changed. Thus, *chien-chien*, straight lines with circles, is read first as 1, then as *kun-kun*, 2; whereas *chien-chien*, straight lines without circles, is read only as 1. (*S*, pp. 57–58)

In "Diary: Audience 1966," the first hexagram (see Figure 1) corresponds to number sixty-three on the chart and is placed first, next to the roman numeral I. The next hexagram is thirty.[33] However, since the first hexagram has a changing line in the *li* trigram (straight, broken, straight), it changes that trigram to *chien* (straight, straight, straight) to form the *chien-kan* hexagram of five. In like fashion, thirty becomes twenty-one to form the first large part of the "Diary."[34] Consequently, it is a reading of the changing lines that enables thirteen hexagrams to produce twenty-one numbers. Symmetrical alteration (four texts, part I;

DIARY: AUDIENCE 1966

I. Are we an audience for computer art? The answer's not No; it's Yes. What we need is a computer that isn't labor-saving but which increases the work for us to do, that puns (this is McLuhan's idea) as well as Joyce revealing bridges (this is Brown's idea) where we thought there weren't any, turns us (my idea) not "on" but into artists. Orthodox seating arrangement in synagogues. Indians have known it for ages: life's a dance, a play, illusion. Lila. Maya. Twentieth-century art's opened our eyes. Now music's opened our ears. Theatre? Just notice what's around. (If what you want in India is an audience, Gita Sarabhai told me, all you need is one or two people.) II. He said: Listening to your music I find it provokes me. What should I do to enjoy it? Answer: There're many ways to help you. I'd give you a lift, for instance, if you were going in my direction, but the last thing I'd do would be to tell you how to use your own aesthetic faculties. (You see? We're unemployed. If not yet, "soon again 'twill be." We have nothing to do. So what shall we do? Sit in an audience? Write criticism? Be creative?) We used to have the artist up on a pedestal. Now he's no more extraordinary than we are. III. Notice audiences at high altitudes and audiences in northern countries tend to be attentive during performances while audiences at sea-level or in warm countries voice their feelings whenever they have them. Are we, so to speak, going south in the way we experience art? Audience participation? (Having nothing to do, we do it nonetheless; our biggest problem is finding scraps of time in which to get it done. Discovery. Awareness.) "Leave the beaten track. You'll see something never seen before." After the first performance of my piece for twelve radios, Virgil Thomson said, "You can't do that sort of thing and expect people to pay for it." Separation. IV. When our time was given to physical labor, I needed a stiff upper lip and backbone. Now that we're changing our minds, intent on things invisible, inaudible, we have other spineless virtues: flexibility, fluency. Dreams, daily events, everything gets to and through us. (Art, if you want a definition of it, is criminal action. It conforms to no rules. Not even its own. Anyone who experiences a work of art is as guilty as the artist. It is not a question of sharing the guilt. Each one of us gets all of it.) They asked me about theatres in New York. I said we could use them. They should be small for the audiences, the performing areas large and spacious, equipped for television broadcast for those who prefer staying at home. There should be a cafe in

FIGURE 2.

three texts, part II; four texts, part III; three texts, part IV; four texts, part V; and three texts, part VI) seems likely to have been planned. However, following Cage's previous use of at least a hundred words per structural unit, one discovers that such a relationship is literally produced "by chance."[35]

Although such symmetry, as well as the number of words in each written statement, is chance-derived, little else is. The method of distinguishing between statements (see Figure 2) is the same as with the "Diary: Emma Lake." Each of the six groups has either three or four statements. If there are three statements, they are distinguished by putting the second statement in parentheses. If there are four, the statements are distinguished in two possible ways. First, the initial statement is printed normally, the second is underlined (italicized in the published text), the third is printed normally, and the fourth is in parentheses. Second, the initial statement is printed normally, the second is in parentheses, the third is printed normally, and the fourth is underlined (italicized in the published text). This procedure is both consistent and fair (in the four statements, Cage reverses the pattern of underlining and parentheses); however, these are not necessarily traits of chance-operated results.

The method just described was probably chosen arbitrarily within what has been shown to be a chance-derived formal structure. However, granting that, an analysis of the content placed within this structure shows the composer to be even more actively involved in making choices. Choosing the texts themselves is obvious enough. Cage constructed them in his mind while driving, according to the number of words required. After he had worked them into a form he could remember, he pulled over and wrote them down. According to his written introduction, the text was finished by the time he arrived in Philadelphia. This story seemed so remarkable that David Revill actually comments specifically about it in his biography of Cage: "With characteristic self-discipline, he ascertained at the start of each leg of the journey how many words were needed for the next statement of the text, formulated it and revised it in his head as he drove, pulled over and wrote it down, checked the length of the next statement and drove on. By the time he reached Philadelphia, the piece was finished."[36] This may seem somewhat redundant, since when one looks up the author's reference it is, in fact, the text itself as published in *A Year from Monday*. However, when one compares the stenographic notebook to both Cage's introduction and Revill's biographical elaboration of it, certain things do not add up. If Cage was writing according to the number of words required in each statement, one would assume that the first text in the notebook would correspond to the first hexagram number derived from the *I Ching*, sixty-three. Instead, one finds that the first written text in the notebook is fifty-one. Although part II is close, there is, in fact, no overall correlation between the order of hexagrams drawn on the first notebook page and the order of texts found in the notebook.[37]

It is not likely that Cage really finished the "Diary" by the time he reached Philadelphia; it is even less likely that he wrote it in the way Revill describes. The following is a more likely scenario. Cage formulated certain statements, some of which were directly related to the topic of the conference where the speech was to be delivered ("The Changing Audience for the Changing Arts"). Most of the initial numbers are large—51, 50, 43, 33, 46, and so on; at the very end, there are four numbers left—24, 17, 10, 5 (see Figure 3). And Cage does indeed do these last four in order from large to small (see note 37). Thus, Cage probably began thinking of things either that he wanted to say or that independently came into his head, paying attention to whether these statements were long or short approximately according to the *I Ching* numbers he, in all likelihood, generated before the trip.

How can one know that they were approximations and that Cage did not have an exact number of words in his mind? First, there is a disparity between generated numbers and written texts. The only other possibility is that Cage worked out of another notebook first and later rewrote everything into the notebook found in his archive. This is extremely doubtful. Anyone who visits Cage's archives immediately senses that he appears to have saved everything, and saved it in an orderly fashion. This is particularly true of the materials found in the literary archive at Wesleyan, most of which were eventually published. In all probability, this notebook is what Cage used in first writing down these texts. Looking again at Figure 1, one notices as further confirmation that the numbers listed to the left of the roman numerals are circled. I would suggest that these were circled as Cage completed that particular text. If accepted, this reasoning also helps explain both the four numbers (24, 17, 10, and 5) on the last four pages of the notebook and the fact that neither 10 nor 5 is circled: since these were probably the texts completed last, circling was unnecessary.

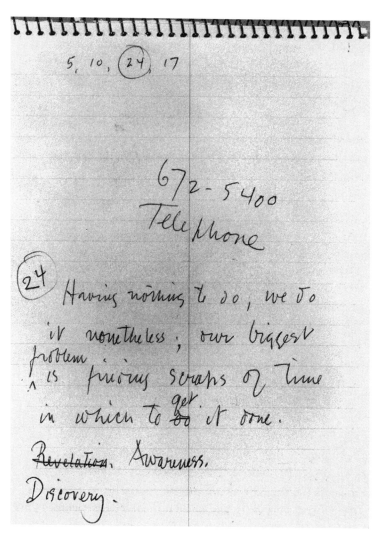

FIGURE 3.

Second, the notebooks show that Cage very carefully edited each of the statements until they did match exactly. And although it is questionable whether he could write as well as edit each of these texts while driving to Philadelphia, such issues, unlike the previous speculations, do not directly affect this analysis. What matters is the editing itself. Figure 4 shows what

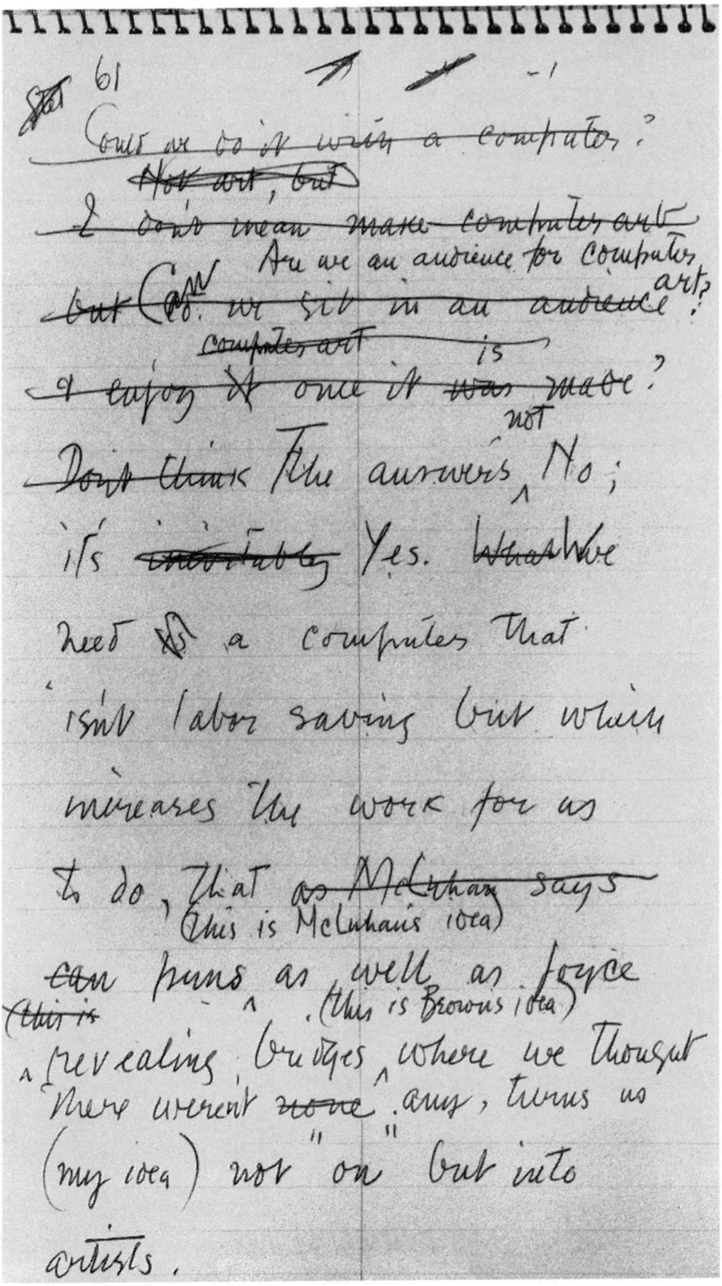

61

Can we do it with a computer?

~~Not art, but~~

~~I don't mean make computer art~~

Are we an audience for computer art?

~~but~~ Can we sit in an audience:

~~computer art~~

~~& enjoy it~~ once it ~~was made~~ is?

~~Don't think~~ The answer is not No;

it's ~~inevitably~~ Yes. ~~What~~ We

need ~~is~~ a computer that

isn't labor saving but which

increases the work for us

to do, that ~~as McLuhan says~~

(this is McLuhan's idea)

~~can~~ puns as well as Joyce

(this is) (this is Brown's idea)

revealing bridges, where we thought

there weren't ~~none~~ any, turns us

(my idea) not "on" but into

artists.

FIGURE 4.

reads as number sixty-one but actually contains sixty-three words and, thus, is the very first statement in the published text. For comparison (and legibility) it is reproduced below, with the text Cage crossed out in brackets.

[Stet] 61
[Could we do it with a computer?]
   [Not art, but]
[I don't mean make computer art]
     Are we an audience for computer art?
[but Can [cd.]³⁸ we sit in an audience]
     [computer art]
[and enjoy [it] once it [was]/is made?]
                     not
[Don't think] T[t]he answer's No;
it's [inevitably] Yes. [What] W[w]e
need [is] a computer that
isn't labor saving but which
increases the work for us
to do, that [as McLuhan says]
     (this is McLuhan's idea)
[can] puns as well as Joyce
[this is]   (this is Brown's idea)
revealing bridges where we thought
there weren't [none]. any, turns us
(my idea) not "on" but into
artists.

Compare this to the published text:

I. Are we an audience for computer art? The answer's not No; it's Yes. What we need is a computer that isn't labor-saving but which increases the work for us to do, that puns (this is McLuhan's idea) as well as Joyce revealing bridges (this is Brown's idea) where we thought there weren't any, turns us (my idea) not "on" but into artists.³⁹

The difference is remarkable, and the final result (even if the original somehow seems more poetic) does closely resemble Cage's view of poetry as "formalized" prose.[40] This leads to a question: did Cage edit the text simply to meet the prescribed sixty-three words, or did he also edit for reasons of personal taste? By comparing script and differing ways of crossing out words one can reproduce what Cage originally wrote:

Could we do it with a computer?
I don't mean make computer art
but cd. we sit in an audience
and enjoy it once it was made?
Don't think the answer's No;
it's inevitably Yes. What we
need is a computer that
isn't labor saving but which
increases the work for us
to do, that as McLuhan says
can pun as well as Joyce
revealing bridges where we thought
there were none.

This excerpt, as is, totals seventy-two words. At the top of the page (see Figure 4) one can distinguish two crossed-out numbers to the left of "−1." These numbers are 9 followed by 4. Cage needed to delete nine words from the text reproduced above to reach the required number of sixty-three. It would be very difficult to determine the order in which he made these changes, so I shall point them out as they occur in the text. Cage crosses out all of "Could we do it with a computer? I don't mean make computer art but cd. we sit in an audience and enjoy it once it was made?" and changes it to "Are we an audience for computer art?" The original has twenty-seven words and the change has seven, for a difference of twenty words. This is not exactly a time-saving method of deleting, overall, nine words. It means that Cage would have had to come up with eleven more words had he accepted the change, which seems unlikely.

What if Cage instead began by crossing out unnecessary words as follows, without an alteration of the text: "inevitably," "what," "is," "as McLuhan says," "can," "none." This shows a remarkable similarity to the crossed-out numbers. Removing "inevitably," "what," "is," "can," and "none" leaves four still to be eliminated; removing "as McLuhan says" leaves one. And, although I am by no means a handwriting expert, it also appears to be consistent with Cage's various noticeable styles of crossing out words. If such were the case, by crossing out "Don't think" and adding "not" to make "The answer's not No; it's Yes," Cage would have made a statement with the required sixty-three words:

> Could we do it with a computer?
> I don't mean make computer art
> but cd. we sit in an audience
> and enjoy it once it was made?
> The answer's not No; it's Yes.
> We need a computer that isn't
> labor saving but which increases
> the work for us to do, that puns
> as well as Joyce revealing bridges
> where we thought there weren't.

I believe the evidence indicates that Cage initially made this text and then changed it. It was purposely altered at great additional expense of time, especially considering the fact that he reportedly was in a hurry. The reasons could be several, but two are probable and important to this analysis. First, he may have wished to alter the original meaning: "any, turns us (my idea) not 'on' but into artists" is clearly a text added to suit the addition of "(this is McLuhan's idea)" and "(this is Brown's idea)." Second, he may simply not have liked the results of his initial editing; indeed, one could say that the final version does read "better."

Looking at the whole manuscript, one sees that there are alterations on every page. The five-word passage "Orthodox seating arrangement in synagogues" (see Figure 5) was originally

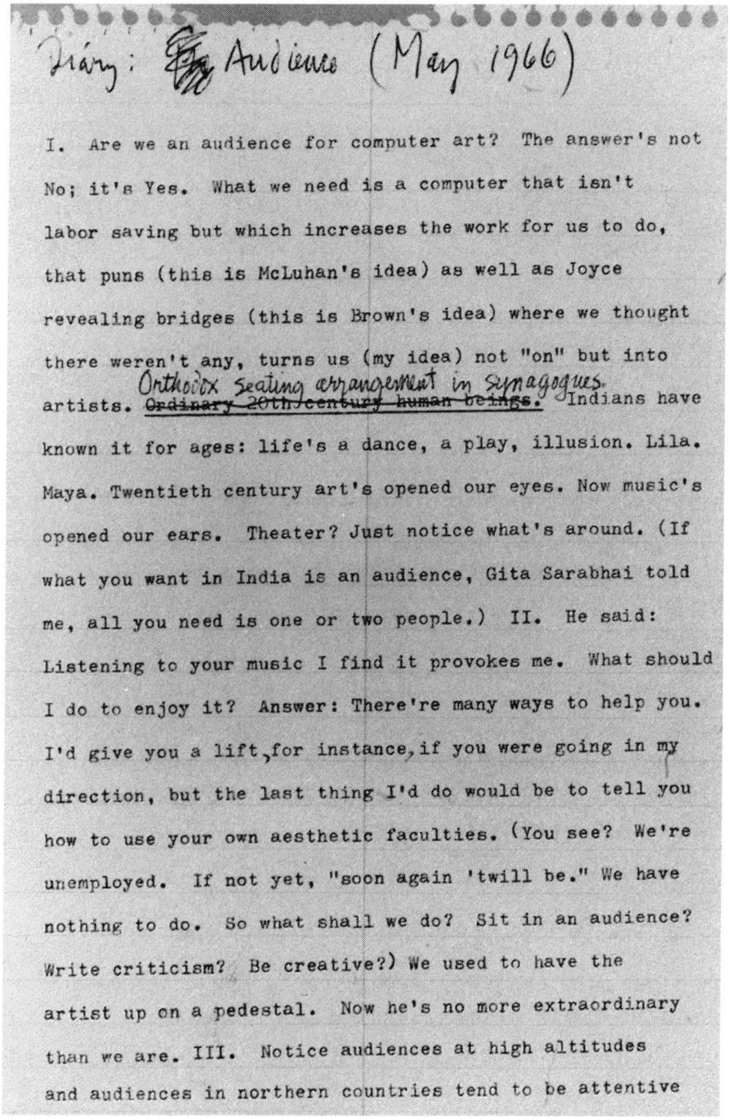

Diary: ~~The~~ Audience (May 1966)

I. Are we an audience for computer art? The answer's not
No; it's Yes. What we need is a computer that isn't
labor saving but which increases the work for us to do,
that puns (this is McLuhan's idea) as well as Joyce
revealing bridges (this is Brown's idea) where we thought
there weren't any, turns us (my idea) not "on" but into
artists. ~~Ordinary 20th century human beings.~~ *Orthodox seating arrangement in synagogues.* Indians have
known it for ages: life's a dance, a play, illusion. Lila.
Maya. Twentieth century art's opened our eyes. Now music's
opened our ears. Theater? Just notice what's around. (If
what you want in India is an audience, Gita Sarabhai told
me, all you need is one or two people.) II. He said:
Listening to your music I find it provokes me. What should
I do to enjoy it? Answer: There're many ways to help you.
I'd give you a lift, for instance, if you were going in my
direction, but the last thing I'd do would be to tell you
how to use your own aesthetic faculties. (You see? We're
unemployed. If not yet, "soon again 'twill be." We have
nothing to do. So what shall we do? Sit in an audience?
Write criticism? Be creative?) We used to have the
artist up on a pedestal. Now he's no more extraordinary
than we are. III. Notice audiences at high altitudes
and audiences in northern countries tend to be attentive

FIGURE 5.

"Ordinary 20th century human beings." In addition, there are
two unused versions of both numbers forty-three and forty-six.
The texts respectively have to do with Cage's mother and with
television. They were, in all likelihood, omitted for the same
reason "Ordinary 20th century human beings" was changed: be-

cause they are not directly related to "audience," the subject of the speech.

Thus what at first seems to be an improvised and haphazard text is actually extremely well organized. Some aspects of form result from chance operations and some do not. The contents, on the other hand, are clearly the result of trying to meet the extraordinary demands of numerical form, subject matter, and personal taste. Even though the juxtapositions, as Cage points out, are derived from chance, the composer's role is so pervasive that the resultant collage of text is, if not completely determined, at least predictable. It is, I would suggest, an immensely taxing exercise of the composer's will, one that does not compare favorably if Cage was trying to produce the kind of non-intention in text that he had already produced in music.

Was Cage in fact trying to produce non-intention in text? His statements lean in that direction. In 1965, for example, he said: "It has been my habit for some years to write texts in a way analogous to the way I write music" (CC, p. 133 [1965]). Yet, as the preceding analysis has shown, analogous means (in this case chance operations) do not necessarily produce similar results. Something more than simply formalized prose was necessary. Cage was looking for a way to "musicate language," as can be seen in the following exchange between him and the French philosopher and musicologist Daniel Charles sometime between 1968 and 1970:

> CHARLES: You propose to musicate language; you want language to be heard as music.
> CAGE: I hope to let words exist, as I have tried to let sounds exist.[41]

An essential aspect of Cage's approach to sound is moving away from memory:

> There is a beautiful statement, in my opinion, by Marcel Duchamp: "To reach the impossibility of transferring from one like object to another the memory imprint." And he

expressed that as a goal. That means, from his visual point of view, to look at a Coca-Cola bottle without the feeling that you've ever seen one before, as though you're looking at it for the very first time. That's what I'd like to find with sounds—to play them and hear them as if you've never heard them before. (*CC*, p. 222 [1984])

The failure of Cage's earlier text pieces was their acceptance of the symbolism that relies upon memory through the syntactical connections and relationships inherent in language. To move away from memory, one must move away from language.

In the mid-1960s Cage found a connection between Duchamp's approach and that of his nineteenth-century predecessor Thoreau:

And that's what links me the most closely with Duchamp and Thoreau. In both of them, as different as they may be, you find a complete absence of interest in self expression. Thoreau wanted only one thing: to see and hear the world around him.[42] When he found himself interested in writing, he hoped to find a way of writing which would allow others not to see and hear how he had done it, but to see *what* he had seen and to hear *what* he had heard. He was not the one who chose his words. They came to him from what there is to see and hear. You're going to tell me that Thoreau has a definite style. He has his very own way of writing. But in a rather significant way, as his *Journal* continues, his words become simplified or shorter. The longest words, I would be tempted to say, contain something of Thoreau in them. But not the shortest words. They are words from common language, everyday words. So, as the words become shorter, Thoreau's own experiences become more and more transparent. They are no longer his own experiences. It is *experience*. And his work improves to the extent that he disappears. He no longer speaks, he no longer writes; he lets things speak and write as they are. I have tried to do nothing else in music. Subjectivity no longer comes into it.[43]

Cage considered this a movement away from memory, from symbolism, in a way that strikingly resembles a common phrase quite familiar to Americanists. It in fact serves as a chapter heading in F. O. Matthiessen's *American Renaissance:* "The Word One with the Thing." As Matthiessen puts it: "The epitome of Emerson's belief is that 'in good writing, words become one with things.'" This then leads to a discussion of organic unity, in which symbolism plays an essential role. Consequently, it is the use of these words that differs and, in this case, leads one away from Matthiessen's Emerson, "where the object is lost in the thought,"[44] and toward Thoreau, who, Cage believed, was moving away from thought and toward the experience of the object in and of itself. And it is the example of Thoreau that showed Cage a way of "musicating language":

CHARLES: If I may now transpose everything you just said to the area of *language,* it seems to me that Thoreau is no less fascinating when he writes, when he frees words. Isn't he concerned with opening up words? And haven't you taken up this concern in turn? Aren't your lectures, for example, musical works in the manner of the different chapters of *Walden*?

CAGE: They are when sounds are words. But I must say that I have not yet carried language to the point to which I have taken musical sounds. I have not yet made noise with it. I hope to make something other than language from it.

CHARLES: How do you expect to accomplish that?

CAGE: It is that aspect, the *impossibility of language,* that interests me at present. I am now working on that problem in a text taken straight from the *Song Books,* which deals directly with letters, syllables, etc., mixing them in such a way that you could call it a *Thoreau Mix.*[45]

This piece eventually came to be called "Mureau," the title being a combination of "music" and "Thoreau." Cage discusses it in the foreword to *M:* "*Mureau* departs from conventional syntax. It is a mix of letters, syllables, words, phrases, and sentences. I wrote it by subjecting all the remarks of Henry David Thoreau about music, silence, and sounds he heard that are indexed in the Dover publication of the *Journal* to a series of I Ching chance operations."[46] The title indicates that Cage was, as he suggests in his conversation with Charles, looking to find a way to take the *Journal* of Thoreau and somehow "musicate it." His first step was to remove syntax: "As we move away from it, we demilitarize language."[47]

Removing syntax would allow words to do what Cage believed Thoreau was trying to have them do: "Since words, when they communicate, have no effect, it dawns on us that we need a society in which communication is not practiced, in which words become nonsense as they do between lovers, in which words become what they originally were: trees and stars and the rest of [the] primeval environment" (*EW*, "The Future of Music," p. 184). Language would move in the direction of the observation of things. Thus, in parallel with his view that music does not communicate, Cage tried to make a language that does not communicate: "The demilitarization of language: a serious musical concern" (*EW*, "The Future of Music," p. 184).

However, Cage realized that "Mureau" had not yet made music out of language; there was still too much language in it and not enough silence:

> sparrowsitA g^ROsbeak betrays *itself* by that peculiar squeakari-
> EFFECT OF SLIGHTEst tinkling measures soundness ingpleasa We
> hear! Does it not rather hear us? sWhen he hears th*e* telegraph,
> he thinksthose bugs have issu*e*d forthThe owl *to*uches the
> stops, wakes reverberations *d gwalky* In verse there is no in-
> herent mus*i*c[48]

In these first few lines of "Mureau," the chance-operated mixture of letters, syllables, words, and sentences goes far beyond the chance operations used to make Cage's "Diaries." But "Mureau" still makes sense. Individual words tend to be read as sentences even when those sentences are devised by the reader rather than by Thoreau. Syllables tend to sound as interruptions of thought rather than as capable of thought, or, as with individual letters, they simply tend to attach themselves to other words, syllables, or letters. Granting that "Mureau" is still interesting poetry, it does not accomplish what Cage had in mind: "I think we need to have more *nonsense* in the field of language" (*CC*, p. 137 [1971]). He therefore continued to search for a verse that *had* what he could regard as "inherent music." This led to the creation of what I regard as one of Cage's finest poetic works, "Empty Words."

"Empty Words" was written in 1973 and 1974. According to Revill, the title was inspired by a conversation with William McNaughton. In 1973, he "told Cage that the classical Chinese language can be classified into 'full words' and 'empty words.' A full word has a specific, in a loose sense referential, meaning; nouns, verbs, adjectives, adverbs, are full words, though which of these forms the word takes cannot always be determined. Empty words are conjunctions, particles, pronouns, which refer only to other terms: a, at, it."[49]

In his introduction to the first part, Cage describes the direction of his work leading to the creation of "Empty Words": hearing Wendell Berry read aloud from the *Journal* in 1967, the importance of Thoreau in his composition *Songbooks* (1970), and the use of chance operations in "Mureau" (*EW*, p. 11). Chance, as in all of Cage's compositions that use it, alters the composer's role from one of making choices to one of asking questions:

> My composition arises out of asking questions. I am reminded of a story early on about a class with Schoenberg. He had us go to the blackboard to solve a particular problem in counterpoint (though it was a class in harmony). He said, "When you have a solution, turn around and let me see it." I did that. He then said, "Now another solution please." I gave another and another until finally, having made seven or eight, I reflected a moment and then said with some certainty: "There aren't any more solutions." He said: "O.K. What is the principle underlying all of the solutions?" I

couldn't answer his question; but I had always worshipped the man, and at that point I did even more. He ascended, so to speak. I spent the rest of my life, until recently, hearing him ask that question over and over. And then it occurred to me through the direction that my work has taken, which is renunciation of choices and the substitution of asking questions, that the principle underlying all of the solutions that I had given him was the question that he had asked, because they certainly didn't come from any other point. He would have accepted that answer, I think. The answers have the question in common. Therefore the question underlies the answers. (*CC*, p. 215 [1980])[50]

Both "Mureau" and "Empty Words" begin with the same question: "What can be done with the English language? Use it as material. Material of five kinds: letters, syllables, words, phrases, sentences. A text for a song can be a vocalise: just letters. Can be just syllables, just words; just a string of phrases; sentences. Or combinations of letters and syllables (for example), letters and words, et cetera. There are 25 possible combinations. Relate 64 (I Ching) to 25. . . . (*Mureau* uses all twenty-five possibilities.)" (*EW*, p. 11). On the other hand—and this is of key significance—"Empty Words" does not use all twenty-five. In the first part, Cage, without using chance operations, eliminated the possibility of sentences by choice:[51] "as we start Lecture One of *Empty Words*, we have no sentences. Though they did exist in *Mureau*, now they've gone" (*CC*, p. 143 [1979]).[52] The difference is striking:

    notAt evening
        right can see
           suited to the morning hour
              trucksrsq Measured tSee t A
        ys sfOi w dee e str oais
           stkva o dcommoncurious 20
    theeberries flowere r clover   (*EW*, p. 12)

In "Mureau," chance operations led to an almost flowing sentence structure, whereas in "Empty Words," because of the elimination of sentences, the text becomes much more disjunct. If phrases, they appear as phrases; if words, as words. This illustrates in text what Cage once said about music: "I try to approach each sound as *itself*" (*CC*, p. 227 [1969]). Owing to Cage's purposeful subtraction of sentences, each phrase, word, syllable, and letter begins to be read "as itself."

Another clue to Cage's intentions was his inclusion in "Empty Words" of drawings by Thoreau, which he describes in the introduction to part one: "Amazed (1) by their beauty, (2) by fact I had not (67–73) been seeing 'em as beautiful, (3) by running across Thoreau's remark: 'No page in my *Journal* is more suggestive than one which includes a sketch.' Illustrations out of context. Suggestivity. Through a museum on roller skates. Cloud of Unknowing. Ideograms. Modern art. Thoreau. 'Yes and No are lies: the only true answer will serve to set all well afloat'" (*EW*, p. 11).[53] In "Empty Words," language begins to move in the direction of those above-mentioned illustrations, ideograms that in China, according to Ezra Pound, "still use abbreviated pictures AS pictures, that is to say, Chinese ideogram does not try to be the picture of a sound, or to be a written sign recalling a sound, but it is still the picture of a thing; of a thing in a given position or relation, or of a combination of things. It *means* the thing or the action or situation."[54]

However, the emphasis remains on "begins." For Cage correctly envisioned this text as a "transition from literature to music" (*CC*, p. 140 [1979]). As such, it is a transition in process, where the symbolic nature of language is being subverted. In part one, even though intention is removed through chance operations, words still connect in specifically meaningful ways: "notAt evening," for example, or "suited to the morning hour." For language to exist as sounds exist, it must be something other than just non-intentional—it must cease to intentionally "mean." This is the process that Cage has set in motion.

Part two removes the possibility of phrases. The introduction to this part continues to describe what questions were asked:

First questions; What is being done? for how many times?
... In which volume of the *Journal*'s fourteen is the syllable
to be found? In which group of pages? On which page of this
group? On which line of this page? (*EW*, p. 33)

The questions help to clarify both the immensity of the task and
why it took so long to complete. And yet, the most significant
change in this part is the elimination of phrases, which was not
a chance operation at all:

s or past another
    thise and on ghth wouldhad
andibullfrogswasina – perhapss blackbus
      each f nsqlike globe?

oi for osurprisingy ter spect y-s of
   wildclouds deooa Di from the
ocolorsadby h allb eblei ingselfi foot   (*EW*, p. 34)

Eventually the process is moving away from any intentional
meaning. Cage is directing the reader to the same Tower of Babel
situation he had found in music more than twenty years before:
"the impossibility of language." If it can't communicate, what
can it do? In the introduction to part three, Cage continues to describe the direction of this process:

Searching (outloud) for a way to read. Changing frequency.
Going up and then going down: going to extremes. Establish
(I, II) stanza's time. That brings about a variety of tempi
(short stanzas become slow; long become fast). (*EW*, p. 51)

Measurement continues through the selection of tempi, but the
reader's role begins to change; he or she searches "outloud for a
way to read."[55] After having "gone to extremes" in parts one and
two, Cage instructs the reader to move "toward a center" in parts
three and four: "To bring about quiet of IV (silence) establish no
stanza time in III or IV" (*EW*, p. 51).

In part three, Cage omits the possibility of words. However, the structures overlap: "E.g., 'a' is a letter, is a syllable, is a word" (*EW*, p. 33). Thus, as the opening to part three demonstrates, "empty" words are not yet fully empty: "the," "perch," "great," "hind," "ten," and so on. Are these ideograms? Or are they still symbols of things rather than the "things themselves"? Is this the nondualism Cage produced in his *Variations III*? Even when removing all but syllables and letters, the text still linguistically "means":

theAf perchgreathind and ten

                    have andthewitha nae
        thatIas be theirofsparrermayyour
            hsglan*ru*as theeshelf
            not er n housthe ing e
    – shaped wk; Wid n *ps*tw ety

    bou-a the dherlyth gth db tgn – plh ng
    sthrce ght rc t e Tm*st*tht thsno sngly o
    ophys thepfbbe ndnd tsh m ie ghl
            ldsbdfrrtlybflyf Ir i q oss bns   (*EW*, p. 52)

I think Cage realized that making the "word one with the thing" was not enough. Nor was the increased semantic openness of language achieved through the use of ideograms a satisfactory solution. For Cage, the only possibility in the midst of this impossibility called language was a new language. And this new language required the same silence *4'33"* had provided in music; the absence of any (even inherently, as in language) intentional meaning. In a 1958 interview with the journalist Mike Wallace, Cage addressed this very issue:

CAGE: Those artists for whom I have regard have always put their work at the service of religion or of metaphysical truth. And art without meaning, like mine, is also at the service of metaphysical truth. But it puts it

in terms which are urgent and meaningful to a person
of this century.

WALLACE: Meaningful? But you said it *has* no meaning.

CAGE: But I mean *no* meaning *has* meaning.

WALLACE: Oh?

CAGE: Yes. This idea of no idea is a *very* important idea.[56]

For Cage, "no meaning" still had meaning. As demonstrated
in conversation with Richard Kostelanetz, empty words are
empty not of meaning but of intentional meaning:

CAGE: I'm not being at all scholarly about my use of the
term "empty words." I'm suggesting something more
in line with what I've already told you, namely, the
transition from language to music, and I would like
with my title to suggest the emptiness of meaning that
is characteristic of musical sounds.

KOSTELANETZ: That is to say, they exist by themselves.

CAGE: Yes. That when words are seen from a musical
point of view, they are all empty.

KOSTELANETZ: They're empty semantically?

CAGE: How do you mean?

KOSTELANETZ: "Semantic" refers to meaning. They are
also empty syntactically.

CAGE: I would rather say that they're empty of intention.
(*CC*, pp. 141–142 [1979])

To remove intention requires omitting even the ideogrammic
nature of language. It requires a complete removal of *all* symbolic reference: "I'm always amazed when people say, 'Do you
mean it's just sounds?' How they can imagine that it's anything
but sounds is what's so mysterious."[57] Sounds thus refer to
themselves rather than to a humanly constructed relationship
between sounds and what they can mean. Languages, too, are
humanly constructed symbolic relationships, and Cage's intention in part four—accomplished, once again, by choice rather

than by chance—was to remove any trace of that symbolic relationship: "IV: equation between letters and silence. Making language saying nothing at all," and finally: "Languages becoming
musics" (EW, pp. 51, 65):

<pre>
ie thA   h   bath
       i   c r   t   t l m rdt   et shgg
           o   no   d   an
           s n   i
   er   t s   p rt oo s
         spwlae   sbr   (EW, p. 66)
</pre>

Cage's "Lecture on Nothing" announced his intent—"I
have nothing to say and I am saying it." "Empty Words," in a way
that has long typified his successful experiments, exemplifies
that intent—"Making language saying nothing at all." As Marjorie Perloff has observed, "In Cage's art of 'exemplary presentation,' the meaning inferred is that we can only know *how* things
happen ('nature in her manner of operation') but never quite
what happens, much less *why*."[58]

"Empty Words" also exemplifies the essential role of the
creator even when the goal is a "silenced" creative self. Cage
used chance operations to open up the creative process, to allow
the "outside" into the work of art. As I have shown, although
chance operations let the "outside" in, they do not, in and of
themselves, necessarily produce "silence." It required an intentional choice—the successive removal of sentences, phrases,
words and syllables—to produce textual silence. In other words,
something (intention) and nothing (non-intention) are not really
opposed; they do "need each other to keep on going" (S, "Lecture
on Something," p. 129). Cage's work, therefore, is not an abdica-
tion but rather a redirection of the role of the artist: "I believe
that by eliminating purpose, what I call *awareness* increases.
Therefore my purpose is to remove purpose" (CC, p. 216 [1961]).
That "purposeful purposelessness" attempts to remove human
constructions of meaning, thus affording awareness of the world
around us the opportunity to increase. Making, then, need not

mean in itself; it may instead open a clearing where, as Robert Duncan has remarked, "We do not make things meaningful, but in our making we work towards an awareness of meaning."[59] The result is the creation of a place where distinctions between text and music disappear, and where, as Charles Olson described it in *Causal Mythology*, "that which exists through itself is what is called meaning."[60]

In "Empty Words," music and text become one. In fact, its greatest significance is in exemplifying the act of becoming: "how things happen." As in Thoreau's *Walden*, Cage takes readers from where they are, a world in which language communicates, and very gradually (the piece takes more than ten hours to perform) moves them to a place where language disappears and words do indeed become "just sounds." In fact, the lecture ends as *Walden* ends, at dawn: "I thought of it as something that could be read through the whole night . . . timing the last part, which is nothing but silences and letters, so that it would end at dawn along with the opening of the windows and doors of the world outside. . . . I have become through *Empty Words* aware of the dawn" (*CC*, p. 124 [1975]). In "Empty Words," Cage "opens words" as Thoreau did, allowing them the freedom to mean apart from symbolic intent, from their human construction. As Thoreau put it, "There is more day to dawn."[61] In other words, there is more than our present experience of it, and by emptying these words of all linguistic intention one may then be open to an experience that includes the outside: " 'to quiet the mind thus making it susceptible to divine influences' " (*CC*, p. 41 [1966]), which is, not surprisingly, what in Cage's view replaced communication as the purpose of writing music.

This book has presented a context by which John Cage can be placed in the disciplines of poetry and music. Within the experimental tradition, I have drawn specific distinctions concerning the role of the self in the creative act. These concern a predilection toward either control or coexistence in two manifestations: the relation between humanity and nature (in essence, either toward the self or away from the self: intention versus non-intention), and nondualism as being pre-existent versus an initial dualism reconciled through humanly contrived unity (either for or against idealism, harmony, symbolism, memory).

It has been the work of John Cage himself that provided the evidence necessary to establish such context. In both his writings and compositions, Cage devoted himself to an aesthetic of coexistent inclusion. By comparing his texts and music, one discovers a shared direction away from compositional control and toward non-intention, where "something" and "nothing" are unopposed. Cage accomplished this first in music, with *4'33"* (1952) and *Variations III* (1962–1963). He then proceeded to accomplish the same result in his texts. By attempting to "musicate" language, Cage eventually moved away from syntactically controlled meaning altogether, and language became, like music, just sounds.

In the introduction to "Empty Words," Cage wrote that "a text for a song can be a vocalise: just letters" (*EW*, p. 11).[62] In "Empty Words," he produced that text, one where language, intentionally stripped of the dualities of its symbolism, becomes unintentional, and thus silenced, song.

Everybody	has a song	
which is	no	song at all :
it is a process	of singing	,
and when you sing	,	
you are	where you are	.

All I know about method is that when I am not working I sometimes think I know something, but when I am working, it is quite clear that I know nothing. (*S*, "Lecture on Nothing," p. 126)

NOTES

INTRODUCTION

1. Jonathan Brent, preface to Peter Gena and Jonathan Brent, eds., *A John Cage Reader in Celebration of His 70th Birthday* (New York: C. F. Peters, 1982), p. xi.

2. Recent Ives scholarship may be outlining a similar distinction between American and European views. In Geoffrey Block and J. Peter Burkholder, eds., *Charles Ives and the Classical Tradition* (New Haven: Yale University Press, 1996), Burkholder, an American, writes: "Ives

sought not to overthrow the great European tradition but to join it as a continuing spirit. In fulfilling this aim, Ives placed himself in the mainstream of European art music in his time" (p. 8). The emphasis here is meant to diminish the view of Ives as "a quintessentially American composer, one who rejected the European tradition and struck out on a new path" (p. 1). On the other hand, David Nicholls, who is British, in a review of several American Ives publications (including *Charles Ives and the Classical Tradition*) asserts: "To establish Ives's compositional pedigree—both American and European—is important. . . . But there is a danger of going too far; of appearing to wish to legitimize his work through association with European tradition. . . . What attracts us to Ives's music is its difference." David Nicholls, "The Great American Borrower," in *Times Literary Supplement*, October 18, 1996, p. 19. My emphasis here concerns what constitutes the process of legitimacy in either Cage or Ives; in Europe, at least, it has always concerned their "American-ness."

3. John Cage with Daniel Charles, *For the Birds* (London: Marion Boyars, 1981), p. 93.

4. John Cage, "Two Statements on Ives," in *A Year from Monday: New Lectures and Writings* (Middletown, Conn.: Wesleyan University Press, 1967), p. 37. According to Stuart Feder, such was also likely the case with Ives, who "used Emerson and his ideas as a vehicle for integrating and organizing ideas of his own." Stuart Feder, *Charles Ives: "My Father's Song": A Psychoanalytic Biography* (New Haven: Yale University Press, 1992), p. 261.

5. Obviously, an interest in experiment is a basic concern of any artist working within the "experimental tradition," and, as such, could be regarded as what defines that tradition. Instead of attempting to initially fix such definitions, a difficult task in and of itself, this book will clarify certain distinctions within the experimental tradition (broadly defined).

6. Thomas DeLio's writings show process as central to experimental traditions in several artistic disciplines. Thomas DeLio, *Circumscribing the Open Universe* (New York: University Press of America, 1984), is but one example. His work has allowed me the latitude of assuming this emphasis on process, thus enabling me to concentrate on distinctions of self within the American experimental tradition.

7. John Cage, "Diary: How to Improve the World (You Will Only Make Matters Worse) Continued 1968 (Revised)," in *M: Writings, '67–'72* (Middletown, Conn.: Wesleyan University Press, 1973), p. 7.

8. Richard Kostelanetz, *Conversing with Cage* (New York: Limelight Editions, 1988), p. 25. Because this book collects different interviews from several sources over many years, I will always include, fol-

lowing the page number, the date of the interview (in this case, 1985).

9. John Cage, "Diary . . . Continued 1968 (Revised)," in *M*, p. 18.

10. John Cage, *I–VI* (Cambridge: Harvard University Press, 1990), pp. 95–96 (punctuation added).

11. Betty E. Ch'maj, "The Journey and the Mirror: Emerson and the American Arts," in *Prospects*, vol. 10 (1985), p. 396.

12. Henry Cowell and Sidney Cowell, *Charles Ives and His Music* (1955; reprint, New York: Da Capo Press, 1983), p. 4.

13. George J. Leonard has performed a similar task in his *Into the Light of Things: The Art of the Commonplace from Wordsworth to John Cage* (Chicago: University of Chicago Press, 1994). According to Leonard, "When Wordsworth declared art to be 'but a handmaid,' he already had in mind what he called 'the blissful hour' when the handmaid's work would be done, all commonplace life transfigured, and the audience lifted to a plane from which it could see all mere real things as miracles" (pp. 25–26). Leonard goes on to proclaim that "John Cage's famous 'silent piece,' *4'33"*, signaled the 'blissful hour's' arrival" (p. 26). I will show that Cage's intentions were opposed to such "transfigurations," which present a dualistic separation between real things and their experience as "miracles." In fact, such dualistic separations are part and parcel of what Emersonian "correspondence" attempts to reconcile. That said, I wish to declare my emphasis on describing the nature and context of Cage's intentions, whether actualized or not. Leonard's point of view and others like it (Daniel Herwitz, *Making Theory/Constructing Art: On the Authority of the Avant-Garde* [Chicago: University of Chicago Press, 1993], pp. 140–173, and Joan Retallack, "Poethics of a Complex Realism," in Marjorie Perloff and Charles Junkerman, eds., *John Cage: Composed in America* [Chicago: University of Chicago Press, 1994], pp. 242–273) suggest an important question: what is criticism addressing, the compositional intent or the heard result of those intentions? Intention and result in Cage's work are not always the same. Leonard's opinion regarding *4'33"* is similarly addressed by both Herwitz and Retallack: the piece is a transformation of experience that requires a willed act on the part of the listener regardless of the composer's desire to remove willed intention from the listening experience.

14. Two general texts that emphasize Emerson's importance are Roy Harvey Pearce, *The Continuity of American Poetry* (1961; reprint, Middletown, Conn.: Wesleyan University Press, 1987), and, especially, Hyatt H. Waggoner, *American Poets from the Puritans to the Present* (1968; rev. ed., Baton Rouge: Louisiana State University Press, 1984). I will cite both specifically elsewhere in this book.

15. H. Daniel Peck, *Thoreau's Morning Work: Memory and Perception in "A Week on the Concord and Merrimack Rivers,"* the *Journal*

and *"Walden"* (New Haven: Yale University Press, 1990), also connects Thoreau, as I will, with the objectivists: "Thoreau is a writer who, because of a unique mixture of predilection and ideas, stands at the threshold of an objectivist, process-oriented philosophy, even though he did not fully comprehend the radical implications of his morning work" (p. xi). As I will demonstrate, one of the very first to comprehend those "radical implications" was John Cage.

16. Kostelanetz, *Conversing with Cage,* p. 55 (1965): "[T]he final picture is of a big fat man, with a smile on his face, returning to the village bearing gifts. He returns without ulterior motive, but he returns. The idea being that after the attainment of nothingness one returns again into activity."

17. John Cage, introduction to *Themes and Variations* (Barrytown, N.Y.: Station Hill Press, 1982) (unpaged).

18. James W. Pritchett, "The Development of Chance Techniques in the Music of John Cage: 1950–1956" (Ph.D. diss., New York University, 1988), p. 5. Later, James Pritchett, *The Music of John Cage* (Cambridge: Cambridge University Press, 1993), continues to emphasize Cage's work as a composer: "because he was primarily a composer— his work in poetry and art inevitably came back into his music, providing him with ideas and themes for new compositions" (p. 175). Although I generally agree with Pritchett's insightful criticism as it specifically applies to Cage's music, I will look at Cage as both writer and composer by making connections between his music and texts that point to the importance of analysis that equally addresses both.

19. Kostelanetz, *Conversing with Cage,* p. 19 (1978).

20. John Cage, *Silence: Lectures and Writings* (Middletown, Conn.: Wesleyan University Press, 1961), p. ix.

21. The "Lecture on Nothing," is a good example. In it, Cage uses "square root form," a structure often found in his music before he introduced chance procedures. I will address this structure in the fourth chapter.

22. Cage, *Silence,* p. x.

23. Kostelanetz, *Conversing with Cage,* p. 133 (1965).

24. Cage, "Mureau," in *M,* p. 35; "Empty Words," in *Empty Words: Writings '73–'78* (Middletown, Conn.: Wesleyan University Press, 1979) p. 11.

INTRODUCTION TO PART ONE

1. Peter Yates claims to have first used the term "American Experimental Music Tradition," and he writes of Ives as the father of this movement in Yates, *Twentieth-Century Music: Its Evolution from the*

End of the Harmonic Era into the Present Era of Sound (New York: Pantheon Books, 1967), p. 269 and p. 258. He also finds nineteenth-century literary roots for this tradition, although he cites Whitman and Melville (p. 62) instead of Emerson and Thoreau.

2. Charles Ives, *"Essays before a Sonata," "The Majority," and Other Writings,* Howard Boatwright, ed. (New York: W. W. Norton, 1970), p. viii.

3. Note that the "discovery" of America (as a literary and artistic theme) occurs at about the same time as what has been called the "new science." Experimentalism (which is partly what made the "new science" new) found social and religious equivalents in a "new world" that, in itself, was thought of as an experiment pursued by a people on an "errand into the wilderness." Tracing such roots is beyond the scope of this book. However, it would be unwise to discuss the issue of experiment without acknowledging its original and lasting importance to American history, particularly as that history intersects with American artistic expression.

4. Waggoner, *American Poets from the Puritans to the Present,* p. xix. David Nicholls describes this same distinction in the discipline of music: "[A] national musical consciousness began to emerge in America. Subsequently, as composers increasingly turned away from Europe, this took many forms. Of these, by far the most consistent and stimulating has been that of experimentalism: consequently, Europeans nowadays often look to America as a major source of new musical ideas." David Nicholls, *American Experimental Music, 1890–1940* (Cambridge: Cambridge University Press, 1990), p. 1.

5. Wilfred Mellers notes this connection in the music of Ives: Mellers, *Music in a New Found Land: Themes and Developments in the History of American Music* (New York: Alfred A. Knopf, 1965). He was also the first writer to connect Thoreau (briefly and unfavorably) with John Cage (pp. 194–195). Gilbert Chase addresses Ives's Emersonian roots even earlier (first ed., 1955) in Chase, *America's Music: From the Pilgrims to the Present,* rev. 3d ed. (Urbana: University of Illinois Press, 1987). Both writers were influenced by *Charles Ives and His Music,* by Henry and Sidney Cowell, the first book to mention a relationship between Emerson and Ives.

6. Cowells, *Charles Ives and His Music,* pp. 7–8: "For his own creed Ives drew on Emerson, and on the uncomfortable Thoreau for courage; it is not too much to say that all his life he has been closer to these two than to any living man. . . . [T]he music most naturally in accord with the eager, independent, and vehemently idealistic New England temper did not emerge until the turn of the century when, between 1896 and 1916 for the most part, Charles Edward Ives set his sweeping and emphatic notes on paper. By that time Emerson's thinking

had been shaping American minds for more than sixty years, without affecting the practice of music at all." J. Peter Burkholder has written, in response to the Cowells' views, that transcendentalism was not a lifelong influence and that it should be regarded as the culmination of his aesthetics rather than as an overriding lifelong artistic concern: Burkholder, *Charles Ives: The Ideas Behind the Music* (New Haven: Yale University Press, 1985). His evidence is convincing and deserves mention when considering the Cowells' important biography. However, since this part of my analysis concerns solely Ives's mature aesthetic as found in his writings, *"Essays before a Sonata"* and the *Memos*, John Kirkpatrick, ed. (1972; reprint, New York: W. W. Norton, 1991), the Cowells and Burkholder are equally beneficial to this study.

7. On the other hand, H. Wiley Hitchcock disagrees: "The greatest influence on his [Ives's] life, his thought, and his music was that of his father George Ives." Hitchcock, *Ives: A Survey of the Music* (1977; reprint, Brooklyn: Institute for Studies in American Music, 1985), p. 5. A biography of Ives by Stuart Feder provides an analysis that better suits the complex relationship between Charles Ives, his father, and Emerson: "Ives's personal 'canonization of Emerson' contains within it the private hagiography of his father. . . . Embedded in Ives's exalted admiration of Emerson is the transformed image of the father and Ives's fused identification with both men." Feder, *Charles Ives: "My Father's Song,"* p. 266.

8. In 1932, Arthur Christy wrote: "we may safely assume that Thoreau and Alcott were in essential agreement with Emersonian doctrine, and that Emerson was a far more comprehensive thinker than they." Christy, *The Orient in American Transcendentalism: A Study of Emerson, Thoreau, and Alcott* (New York: Columbia University Press, 1932), p. 187.

9. See F. O. Matthiessen, *American Renaissance: Art and Expression in the Age of Emerson and Whitman* (New York: Oxford University Press, 1941). Matthiessen saw Thoreau as departing from Emerson via his emphasis on the senses.

10. In the 1960s, Joel Porte expanded upon Matthiessen's view of Thoreau's sensual emphasis in his comparative work *Emerson and Thoreau: Transcendentalists in Conflict* (Middletown, Conn.: Wesleyan University Press, 1966). It is still the best available account of the relationship between the two men. One year later Cage learned of Thoreau from the poet and essayist Wendell Berry.

11. Joel Porte continues to write about Thoreau. See his *In Respect to Egotism: Studies in American Romantic Writing* (Cambridge: Cambridge University Press, 1991). Other scholars in the field include Stan-

ley Cavell, *The Senses of Walden: An Expanded Edition* (1972; reprint, Chicago: University of Chicago Press, 1981); and Jeffrey Steele, *The Representation of the Self in the American Renaissance* (Chapel Hill: University of North Carolina Press, 1987). Walter Harding should be mentioned separately, as he was devoted to the life and work of Thoreau. Walter Harding, *The Variorum "Walden"* (1962; reprint, New York: Washington Square Press, 1963), and Walter Harding and Michael Meyer, *The New Thoreau Handbook* (New York: New York University Press, 1980), are both essentials for Thoreau scholars. All of these writers treat Thoreau and Emerson separately. However, they also consider them as part of a tradition of romanticism that emphasizes the self as an active "reformer" of experience. Consequently, most of these writers serve as citations for Emerson as well. Exceptions include Peck, *Thoreau's Morning Work*; Joan Burbick, *Thoreau's Alternative History: Changing Perspectives on Nature, Culture, and Language* (Philadelphia: University of Pennsylvania Press, 1987); Laura Dassow Walls, *Seeing New Worlds: Henry David Thoreau and Nineteenth-Century Natural Science* (Madison: University of Wisconsin Press, 1995); and especially Sharon Cameron, *Writing Nature: Henry Thoreau's "Journal"* (1985; reprint, Chicago: University of Chicago Press, 1989), a unique critical analysis of Thoreau's *Journal* that, unlike any other available criticism, describes (albeit unintentionally) Thoreau's writings in a way that shares remarkable similarities with the ideas of John Cage.

12. I make the distinction between striving toward monistic unity and achieving it in order to clarify my approach to both Emerson and Ives. In his article "De-Transcendentalizing Emerson," in *ESQ: A Journal of the American Renaissance*, vol. 34, 1st and 2d quarters (1988), Michael Lopez remarks: "Emerson's dualisms were necessary: . . . if the timeless unity which is always postponed were ever attained, the time-bound *drama* of the individual's search for power and a well-grounded self would cease. . . . The paradoxical Emersonian longing for the integration of some kind of religious Unity or vision of an Absolute with a fierce affirmation of autonomous individuality may be characteristically American" (p. 122). It is also most certainly Ivesian.

DUALISM/UNITY/CONTROL

1. Russell B. Goodman, *American Philosophy and the Romantic Tradition* (Cambridge: Cambridge University Press, 1990), p. 52.

2. Ralph Waldo Emerson, *Emerson's Essays* (First and Second Series) (1926; reprint, New York: Harper and Row, 1951), p. 2. (Further

references to this work, abbreviated *EE*, will be included parenthetically in the text of this chapter.)

3. Goodman, *American Philosophy*, p. 52.

4. Ralph Waldo Emerson, *Selected Essays*, Larzer Ziff, ed. (New York: Penguin Books, 1982), p. 236. (Further references to this work, abbreviated *SE*, will be included parenthetically in the text of this chapter.) "Circles" is frequently cited when one wishes to mention the open-ended, experimental nature of Emerson's work. However, my analysis places such experiments firmly within the context of the human self: a "fixed" element in the midst of such open-endedness.

5. Emerson tends to use the words reason and spirit interchangeably, at least in the sense that applies here. Both are permanent and fixed; both lie not within nature but within the human mind.

6. Regarding Emerson's idealism, Stanley Cavell remarks that "moods must be taken as having at least as sound a role in advising us of reality as sense-experience has." Cavell, *The Senses of Walden*, p. 125. Probably *more* of a role: Emerson's idealism places far more weight on intellectual interpretation of the senses than it does the actual sensual experience. Kant's thing-in-itself cannot be known either through concepts or experience: "[H]ow can we know what belongs to things in themselves, since this never can be done by the dissection of our concepts (in analytical propositions)?" and "[E]xperience teaches us what exists and how it exists, but never that it must necessarily exist so and not otherwise. Experience therefore can never teach us the nature of things in themselves." Immanuel Kant, "Second Part of the Main Transcendental Problem: How Is Pure Science of Nature Possible?" in *Prolegomena to Any Future Metaphysics*, Carus translation rev. by Lewis White Beck (Indianapolis: Bobbs-Merrill/Library of Liberal Arts, 1950), p. 42. However, Kant does believe that the nature of things follows natural *a priori* laws; things just cannot be known merely by concepts or experience. Emerson's idealism makes things "knowable," which connects him with post-Kantian philosophy. As I will point out, Thoreau and Cage reject that idealism, eliminate the necessity of "knowing," and operate within the realm of "what" and "how" rather than "why."

7. Only by recognizing the experimental tradition's continuance, and Ives's essential part in it, can the distinction this analysis makes be fully appreciated. Consequently, before showing how Ives perpetuates Emersonian dualism and the controlling self's imposition of unity, both of which are central to his mature aesthetic, I must acknowledge the complexities out of which distinctions of self emerge. For example, Ives and Cage share many similarities. Both credit the influence of their fathers for their inventiveness. Both played percussion instruments (Ives as a boy in his father's band, Cage as a member of a percussion ensemble

he himself formed). Both emphasize process in their work. Both share a compositional concern with the use of collage. Cage and Ives also seem to have formed their aesthetic views independently, seeking confirmation from other sources only after their positions had been determined. Both also have, of course, a deep affection for the writings of Thoreau. However, similar interests do not result in similar uses. According to J. Peter Burkholder, "Ives formulated one principal aim for the works of his maturity: the representation in music of human experience." Burkholder, *Charles Ives*, p. 13. In contrast, Cage (and Thoreau as well) wished to include not just the human experience but *all* experience.

8. Thoreau and Emerson were more closely linked when Ives was forming his aesthetic views. When Cage discovers Thoreau, divisions are beginning to be addressed. Equally important, perhaps, is which of Thoreau's writings attracted Cage and Ives. In his *"Essays before a Sonata,"* Ives quotes extensively from Thoreau's poetry, *Walden*, and *A Week on the Concord and Merrimack Rivers*. He also makes use of two other volumes, one biography and one criticism: Edward Waldo Emerson, *Henry Thoreau: As Remembered by a Young Friend* (Boston: Houghton Mifflin, 1917), and Mark Van Doren, *Henry David Thoreau: A Critical Study* (1916; reprint, New York: Russell and Russell, 1961). Thoreau's *Journal* is cited only once, in a quotation from Van Doren's study. Cage, on the other hand, discovers Thoreau via his *Journal* first, his other writings later. Scholars who see the texts that Ives was most familiar with as primary tend to share his view of continuity between Emerson and Thoreau (at least as the texts concern issues of self). Most scholars who follow Cage's progression of the *Journal* as first (thus coloring the interpretation of his other writings) tend to make distinctions similar to those Cage finds between Emerson and Thoreau, elements that form the distinction of self at the heart of this book. The difference could be partly generational; according to Gary Scharnhorst, "the journal was not published until 1906 and not really canonized until about 1950" (private correspondence, July 1993).

9. Cage especially admired Ives's use of collage and his concern for the spatial positioning of sound sources. He did not appreciate Ives's use of quotation (at least in the *way* Ives intended its use) or the way in which the complexity of Ives's music "emerges" (everyone hearing the same thing) instead of simply allowing the audience to "enter in" ("Everybody hears what he alone hears if he enters in"). Cage, *A Year from Monday*, pp. 36–42. Cage's agreement with Ives moves toward multiplicity and non-intention. His disagreement centers upon issues of symbolism and control, two important aspects of this book.

10. I especially like J. Peter Burkholder's placement of Ives in four

traditions: American popular music, American Protestant church music, European classical music, and experimental music. See Burkholder, "Ives and the Four Musical Traditions," in *Charles Ives and His World,* J. Peter Burkholder, ed. (Princeton: Princeton University Press, 1996), pp. 3–34. I am most obviously interested in this last category, where, as Burkholder writes, Ives "stands at the beginning of a century-long tradition" (p. 4).

11. Nicholls, *American Experimental Music, 1890–1940,* p. 6.

12. Ch'maj, "The Journey and the Mirror," p. 396.

13. Rosalie Sandra Perry, *Charles Ives and the American Mind* (Kent, Ohio: Kent State University Press, 1974), pp. xvii–xviii.

14. Burkholder, *Charles Ives,* p. 8.

15. Ibid.

16. Ives, "Epiloque," in *"Essays before a Sonata,"* p. 74. (Further references to this work, abbreviated *EB,* will be included parenthetically in the text of this chapter.)

17. Burkholder, *Charles Ives,* p. 10.

18. Ives situates Emerson's dual view of humanity and nature through morality, citing his "Compensation": "a story of the analogy, or, better, the identity of polarity and duality in Nature with that in morality" (*EB,* p. 15).

19. Mellers, *Music in a New Found Land,* p. 47.

20. John Cage, on the other hand, disliked Beethoven as much as he disliked Emerson. In his "Defense of Satie" Cage wrote: "With Beethoven the parts of a composition were defined by means of harmony. With Satie and Webern they are defined by means of time lengths. The question of structure is so basic, and it is so important to be in agreement about it, that one must now ask: Was Beethoven right or are Webern and Satie right? I answer immediately and unequivocally, Beethoven was in error, and his influence, which has been as extensive as it is lamentable, has been deadening to the art of music" (quoted in Richard Kostelanetz, ed., *John Cage* [1970; reprint, New York: Da Capo Press, 1991], p. 81). One composer who fell under the "lamentable" influence of Beethoven was Charles Ives, and harmony, as I will demonstrate, is an important area of difference between Cage and Ives.

21. Mellers, *Music in a New Found Land,* p. 48.

22. Cowells, *Charles Ives and His Music,* p. 155.

23. Ibid., p. 154.

24. Ibid., p. 155.

25. Ibid., p. 142.

26. Ibid.

27. Ibid., pp. 142–143.

28. Ch'maj, "The Journey and the Mirror," p. 396.

29. Porte, *Emerson and Thoreau*, p. 63.

30. Ibid., p. 132.

31. Concerning Emerson, see Christopher Collins, *The Uses of Observation: A Study of Correspondential Vision in the Writings of Emerson, Thoreau, and Whitman* (The Hague: Mouton, 1971), p. 53: "There exists a strict dualism of the 'me' and the 'not me'—the central self and the flowing, ambient world of phenomena. Upon this dualism he based his method of poetic mysticism, the method of correspondence."

32. Porte, *Emerson and Thoreau*, p. 12.

33. Ibid., p. 13.

34. Pearce, *The Continuity of American Poetry*, p. 160, p. 159.

35. Julie Ellison, *Emerson's Romantic Style* (Princeton: Princeton University Press, 1984), p. 197.

36. Hitchcock, *Ives: A Survey of the Music*, p. 89.

37. Ives, *Memos*, p. 39. According to Kirkpatrick, only one manuscript page (of the *Postlude*)—and possibly a sketch—survives.

38. Ibid., pp. 61–62.

39. Ibid., p. 96.

40. Charles E. Ives, "Note," in *Central Park in the Dark*, Jacques-Louis Monod, ed., with notes by John Kirkpatrick (Hillsdale, N.Y.: Boelke-Bomart, 1973), p. 31.

41. Charles Ives, *Second Pianoforte Sonata, "Concord, Mass., 1840–1860,"* 2d ed. (New York: Arrow Music Press, 1947).

42. Ives, *Memos*, p. 104.

43. Hitchcock, *Ives: A Survey of the Music*, p. 71.

44. Ives, *Memos*, pp. 97–98.

45. Ibid., p. 64.

46. Perry, *Charles Ives and the American Mind*, p. 65.

47. Ibid.

48. Much scholarship recognizes the important role of memory in the compositional aesthetics of Charles Ives. Some of the most important studies include Feder, *Charles Ives: "My Father's Song"*: "The songs in particular, but in a way Ives's entire work, constitute a singular American autobiography in music. The collection is full of ideas, musical and other, but above all it is full of memories" (p. 2); and David Michael Hertz, *Angels of Reality: Emersonian Unfoldings in Wright, Stevens, and Ives* (Carbondale: Southern Illinois University Press, 1993): "What he [Ives] was after was more than nostalgia. He was not merely sentimentalizing about the past. He was fashioning in music a psychological re-experiencing of the past" (p. 280). J. Peter Burkholder, *All Made of Tunes: Charles Ives and the Uses of Musical Borrowing* (New Haven: Yale University Press, 1995), includes the following about Ives's *Fourth of July*: "When Ives is remembering, one tune will suggest an-

other that resembles it in melody or rhythm, or with which it is associated by common genre or use in similar circumstances. The result is a collage of half-heard and half-remembered tunes that is a wonderfully true musical evocation of the way human memory works" (p. 380).

49. Cage, "Two Statements on Ives," in *A Year from Monday*, p. 41 (punctuation added).

50. Elliott Carter, quoted in Vivian Perlis, *Charles Ives Remembered: An Oral History* (New Haven: Yale University Press, 1974), p. 145.

51. Frank R. Rossiter, *Charles Ives and His America* (New York: Liveright, 1975), p. 157.

52. Larry Starr, *A Union of Diversities: Style in the Music of Charles Ives* (New York: Schirmer Books, 1992), p. 16.

53. Ives, *Memos*, p. 59.

54. Burkholder, *Charles Ives*, p. 13.

55. Ibid., p. 32.

56. Burkholder considers Ives's use of collage to be a less directly representational rendering of experience: "The intended effect in most of Ives's collages is to convey the sense of an event, not as it actually might have happened, as in *Central Park in the Dark* or *Decoration Day*, but as it is remembered or envisioned, with the cloud of borrowed tunes representing memories or thoughts associated with the events being pictured." Burkholder, *All Made of Tunes*, pp. 369–370. I would add only that even Ives's attempts to write music that portrays events as they "actually happened" reside initially in the composer's memory.

57. Perry, *Charles Ives and the American Mind*, p. 65.

58. See Feder, *Charles Ives: "My Father's Song,"* where he writes the following about Ives's song "The Things Our Fathers Loved": "no tune achieves anything approaching full performance; only snatches, fragments, vague allusions are perceived as they might exist in memory" (p. 254).

59. Hitchcock, *Ives: A Survey of the Music*, pp. 51–52. The quotation comes from *EB*, "Epilogue," p. 96.

60. Howard Boatwright attaches the following note to Ives's remark: "Probably not a quotation." He then points to a similar passage in the "Beauty" chapter of Emerson's book *Nature*.

61. Cowells, *Charles Ives and His Music*, pp. 193–194.

62. Hitchcock, *Ives: A Survey of the Music*, pp. 55–56.

63. Perry, *Charles Ives and the American Mind*, p. 51.

64. Starr, *A Union of Diversities*, p. 54.

65. Ch'maj, "The Journey and the Mirror," p. 392.

66. Unlike Ives, Cage wished to diminish the power memory ex-

erts: "Something has to be done to get us free of our memories and choices." Kostelanetz, *Conversing with Cage*, p. 119 (1982).

NONDUALISM AND COEXISTENCE

1. Henry David Thoreau, "Where I Lived and What I Lived For," in *"Walden" and Other Writings*, Brooks Atkinson, ed. (New York: Modern Library, 1937), pp. 81–82. (Also see "Economy," p. 45: "How could youths better learn to live than by at once trying the experiment of living?") (Further references to this work, abbreviated *W*, will be included parenthetically in the text of this chapter.)

2. This is the first occasion where I take issue with Cavell, *The Senses of Walden*. (Further references to this work, abbreviated *SW*, will be included parenthetically in the text of this chapter.) My disagreement concerns the following quotation from *Walden*: "The universe constantly and obediently answers to our conceptions" (*W*, "Where I Lived and What I Lived For," p. 87). Cavell considers this an instance where Thoreau continues the Emersonian tradition of "building your own world." As he sees it, "The writer of *Walden* proposes himself many times and in many ways as the creator of his world" (*SW*, p. 111). I disagree and think the quotation exemplifies the opposite of what Cavell describes. Thoreau is discovering his world, not making it. For him, the world and the life it offers are there already. The universe "answers to our conceptions" only as we experimentally discover them. Since Thoreau's experiment is a question, not a hypothesis, observing the universe is the sole possible "answer." As I read Thoreau, the idea of predetermined human conceptions matching those found in nature is not what he had in mind.

3. *The Senses of Walden* at first seems to resonate with this point of view. I am thinking in particular of the following passage from Cavell's book: "these *a priori* conditions [of knowing objects] are not themselves knowable *a priori*, but are to be discovered experimentally" (p. 95). However, I question the connection Cavell makes between Thoreau and epistemology. It is experience, not knowledge, that I read as being important to Thoreau. Such being the case, he presupposes no *a priori* conditions; he emphasizes discovery, not rediscovery. Consequently, Thoreau's quest is not what Cavell calls a "recovery of the self" (p. 80). "Recovery" presumes an *a priori* and thus pre-existing knowledge of self. The quest is, instead, the previously unknown experiential discovery of self.

4. Emerson, *Selected Essays*, p. 81.

5. Some critics will be quick to insist, however, that Thoreau is

writing *Walden* to "wake his neighbors up," and that, as such, it is not the record of his experiment but his "report." John Cage has remarked that Thoreau "did have a question: Is life worth living? *Walden* is his detailed and affirmative reply." John Cage, "Preface to 'Lecture on the Weather,'" in *Empty Words*, p. 3. *Walden* is Thoreau's attempt at answering the question of living life; however, to participate in his experiment one must look in his *Journal*.

6. Cage, "Experimental Music: Doctrine," in *Silence*, p. 13. (Further references to this work, abbreviated *S*, will be included parenthetically in the text of this chapter.) It is this aspect of Cage's experimentalism that reflects his initial interest in Thoreau's *Journal*. If *Walden* is an "affirmative reply" (see note 5), it would not be experimental in the way Cage defines experiment here. The *Journal*, however, which Sharon Cameron regards as posing questions that remain questions (Cameron, *Writing Nature*, p. 154), better exemplifies Cage's preference for experiments without an evaluative response.

7. "I explained that I'd never been interested in symbolism; that I preferred just taking things as themselves, not as standing for other things" (*S*, p. 85).

8. Cole Gagne and Tracy Caras, *Soundpieces: Interviews with American Composers* (London: Scarecrow Press, 1982), pp. 78–79.

9. Henry David Thoreau, *Journal*, Bradford Torrey and Francis H. Allen, eds. (1906; reprint, New York: Dover Publications, 1962), p. 103 (March 20, 1842). (Further references to this work, abbreviated *J*, will be included parenthetically in the text of this chapter.) I use the Dover rather than the Princeton edition not only because the latter remains unfinished but, more important, because it is the edition Cage used.

10. Emerson, "Idealism," from *Nature*, in *Selected Essays*, p. 64.

11. Gary Scharnhorst discovered a remarkable affirmation of this point of view in Ralph Waldo Emerson's journal. Emerson writes that Thoreau believed "the poem ought to sing itself: if the man took too much pains with the expression he was not any longer the Idea himself." *Emerson in His Journals*, Joel Porte, ed. (Cambridge: Belknap Press of Harvard University Press, 1982), p. 207 (Nov. 10–11, 1838).

12. Peck, *Thoreau's Morning Work*, addresses similar issues. Of particular interest here is his consideration of Steven Owen's studies of Chinese poetry: "Unlike Western poetry, classical Chinese poetry is not heavily dependent on metaphor. Instead, it employs a mode of representation Owen calls 'parallelism': 'Parallelism and metaphor are essentially different: unlike metaphor, parallelism supposes that both terms are present on the same level of discourse and that neither "stands in for" the other. Metaphor subordinates its terms: one points to the other (whether it is known or not). Parallelism is content to let its terms rest

side by side.'" (Quoting Stephen Owen, *Traditional Chinese Poetry and Poetics: Omen of the World* [Madison: University of Wisconsin Press, 1985], p. 96.) Peck then goes on to say: "Thoreau's Journal is not a poetic 'text' in quite the same sense as the works treated in Owen's study. But his heavy use of visual analogy in landscape description strongly suggests the process Owen calls parallelism." And finally: "The force of such parallelisms in the Journal is to bring both objects being compared vividly before our eyes, giving priority to neither, and drawing no special attention to the viewer's act of perception" (pp. 71–72). This section of his book also concerns the connection Peck sees between Thoreau and the objectivists (who will figure prominently in the next chapter). Regarding one of Thoreau's *Journal* entries (July 18, 1851), Peck observes that "[p]erhaps it is the early Williams rather than Pound who comes most immediately to mind here, but the features of poetic language that we associate with imagism are unmistakable" (pp. 70–71). Peck qualifies his earlier observation as follows: "It would be a mistake, however, to apply Owen's distinction broadly to the procedures of Thoreau's Journal. As a romantic writer, Thoreau is often given to the traditional use of metaphor even in this document" (p. 72). And in contrast to my analysis, Peck considers "relation and harmony" to be the "twin objectives of the Journal's unending work" (p. 62), considering his "morning work" to be "most significantly the work of memory and perception as these faculties conjoin to serve Thoreau's emerging vision of cosmos" (p. xi). On the other hand, Peck does consider parallelism as "useful because it suggests an important tendency in Thoreau's thought. Parts of his Journal, especially those parts devoted to landscape description, strive toward an objectivist, presentational view of the world. And this is true, often, even when he is employing metaphor" (p. 72). This important tendency, which Peck calls parallelism and I call coexistence, is what especially attracted Cage to Thoreau.

13. Porte, *In Respect to Egotism*, p. xii.

14. One exception is Sharon Cameron's *Writing Nature*, which sees Thoreau's *Journal* as a writing that moves away from the self in the direction of nature. I once asked her if she was aware of John Cage's affinity for Thoreau's work. She wasn't. I was especially curious because, although there are strong connections between how they both view the writings of Thoreau, Cameron's work differs from Cage's in that she assumes a dualistic relation between humanity and nature. Cameron regards Thoreau's quest toward nature as a tragic one, where his observations remain outside the natural experience. The point is noteworthy since it is Cage's interest in Asian rather than Western philosophy that moves away from dualism (and the Western conception of tragedy that underlies it) into a nondual coexistence between humanity and nature.

It was Cage's opinion, which I emphasize in this book, that Thoreau was also writing from a nondual perspective—that he was writing from within rather than from without nature.

15. Emerson, "Man the Reformer," in *Selected Essays*, p. 142.

16. Ibid., p. 140.

17. Cage put it this way: "Our intention is to affirm this life, not to bring order out of chaos nor to suggest improvements in creation, but simply to wake up to the very life we're living, which is so excellent once one gets one's mind and one's desires out of its way and lets it act of its own accord" (*S*, "In This Day . . . ," p. 95).

18. Emerson, "Prospects," from *Nature*, in *Selected Essays*, p. 81.

19. Emerson, *Selected Essays*, p. 65.

20. Cage, "Preface to 'Lecture on the Weather,'" in *Empty Words*, p. 3.

21. Cameron, *Writing Nature*, p. 11: "What remains is just enough of the human to represent the natural: an isolated man recording his impressions of nature."

22. Emerson, "Nature," from *Nature*, in *Selected Essays*, p. 39.

23. Harding, ed., *The Variorum "Walden,"* p. 287 (Confucius, *The Doctrine of the Mean*, XVI, 1–3).

24. Cameron, *Writing Nature*, p. 48: "[O]nce Thoreau sees that correspondences between nature and the self are incomplete and uncompletable, what he would like to do is to prohibit them entirely. So doing, he would preserve the idea that nature is alien. But my claim is a complex and an apparently contradictory one, for the way Thoreau imagines that nature is alien is by also imagining that he could impersonate the alienness—that he could voice nature or be nature's voice." Cameron, along with Cavell, misses the relationship between being against symbolic reference and nondualism, which is why her argument seems contradictory. Thoreau, by de-centering the self, can allow nature in because there is *no* separation. Nature is not alien; nature and the self are inherently one. By removing symbols, a human method of appropriating nature, it is then possible to experience the nondual character of reality.

25. Cage, *I–VI*, p. 6.

26. Jonathan Brent, "Preface," in Gena and Brent, eds., *John Cage Reader*, pp. x, xi.

27. Cage, "Diary: How to Improve the World (You Will Only Make Matters Worse) Continued 1968 (Revised)," in *M*, p. 18.

28. Cage, "An Autobiographical Statement," in Richard Kostelanetz, ed., *John Cage: Writer: Previously Uncollected Pieces* (New York: Limelight Editions, 1993), p. 237.

29. Cage, "Diary: Audience 1966," in *A Year from Monday*, p. 51.

30. Cage, "Diary: How to Improve the World," in *A Year from Monday*, p. 19. As I will show in the last chapter, this contextual study is leading to the description of ways in which Cage tried to "silence himself" by removing separations between things and thus bringing about nondual experiences. It is also why my analysis ends in the mid-1970s, with "Empty Words." It is of course conceivable that, regardless of his desire to produce nondual experiences (which is all this analysis attempts to prove), Cage never really believed it possible to remove the separations between art and life that hinder the ability to have such experiences. Marjorie Perloff suggests as much when she responds to a conversation between Cage and Moira and William Roth about Marcel Duchamp's *Etant Donnés*. The conversation, which occurred in 1973, as he was writing "Empty Words," includes the following remark by Cage: "So he's telling us something that we perhaps haven't yet learned, when we speak as we do so glibly of the blurring of the distinction between art and life. Or perhaps he's bringing us back to Thoreau: yes and no are lies. Or keeping the distinction, he may be saying neither one is true. The only true answer is that which will let us have both of these" (Kostelanetz, *Conversing with Cage*, p. 180). Perloff's response includes the following point: "the breakdown of the distinction between 'art' and 'life,' which he himself had been theorizing ever since *Silence*, is not as simple as it has seemed to some of his followers and exegetes" (Marjorie Perloff, "'A duchamp unto my self': 'Writing through' Marcel," in Perloff and Junkerman, eds., *John Cage: Composed in America*, p. 117. (Note that Perloff cites Cage's remarks only through "yes and no are lies.") Cage's remarks are twofold, with the reference to Thoreau clearly an example of the coexistence I am describing. His earlier words, however, imply the possibility of separation in a way that supports George J. Leonard's views in this regard. As he sees it, there are "two Cages," one of whom spoke of silence in a way decidedly contrary to the approach considered here: "You might say we wonder whether we have ruined the silence." Leonard, *Into the Light of Things*, p. 176. (Cage made these remarks in a 1990 PBS *American Masters* program about his work.) This describes a situation far different from that of a silenced and coexistent self. But if there are indeed two Cages (and there are likely even more), I wish to clarify here that the Cage who considers the possibility of separations between art and life and a "ruined" silence lies outside and historically after the purview of this analysis: in other words, after the silence itself, in both music and text, is produced.

31. John Cage, in conversation with the author, July 6, 1990.

32. Ives, "Thoreau," in *"Essays before a Sonata,"* p. 51.

33. Kenneth W. Rhoads, "Thoreau: The Ear and the Music," in *American Literature*, vol. 46, no. 3 (November 1974), p. 319.

34. Ibid., p. 320.

35. Ibid., p. 315.

36. Matthiessen, *American Renaissance*, p. 91.

37. William Duckworth, "Anything I Say Will Be Misunderstood: An Interview with John Cage," in Richard Fleming and William Duckworth, eds., *John Cage at Seventy-Five* (Lewisburg, Pa.: Bucknell University Press, 1989), p. 16.

38. Cage, "Foreword," in *M* (unpaged).

39. Emerson, "Nature," from *Nature*, in *Selected Essays*, p. 38.

40. John Cage, unpublished lecture given at the Ferienkurse für Neue Musik, Darmstadt, Germany, July 1990, p. 5.

41. Kostelanetz, *Conversing with Cage*, p. 25 (1985).

42. Ibid., p. 189 (1968).

43. Cage, "Source Text: Nonunderstanding," in *I–VI*, p. 444.

44. Thoreau's "telegraph harp" was the sound made by the wind blowing over telegraph lines.

45. Kostelanetz, *Conversing with Cage*, p. 188 (1968).

46. The sounds of *4'33"* do embody what "Cage and Thoreau regarded as music." However, even though the composer does not will any of the sounds, he does will the structure, or frame, within which those non-intentional sounds exist. Thus, as I will demonstrate in the last chapter, Cage himself considered *4'33"* an unsuccessful attempt at making a nondual musical structure.

47. Cameron, *Writing Nature*, p. 75.

48. Charles Olson, "The View, Part Two: The Topological," in *The Special View of History*, Ann Charters, ed. (Berkeley, Calif.: Oyez, 1970), p. 49.

49. Quoted in Margaret Leng Tan, "'Taking a Nap, I Pound the Rice': Eastern Influences on John Cage," in Fleming and Duckworth, eds., *John Cage at Seventy-Five*, p. 43. Cage writes of having visited Hamada, who said to him, "I'm not interested in results" ("Diary: How to Improve the World (You Will Only Make Matters Worse) 1965," in *A Year from Monday*, p. 6).

50. Kostelanetz, *Conversing with Cage*, p. 231 (1984).

51. Norman O. Brown, "John Cage," in Fleming and Duckworth, eds., *John Cage at Seventy-Five*, p. 110.

52. Sherman Paul, "The Wise Silence: Sound as the Agency of Correspondence in Thoreau," in *New England Quarterly*, vol. 22, no. 4 (December 1949), p. 513.

53. However, it is, as my analysis suggests, moving in the direction of the *Journal*: away from humanly contrived symbolism and toward nondualism.

54. Sherman Paul, "Resolution at Walden" (1953), in Joel Myerson,

ed., *Critical Essays on Henry David Thoreau's "Walden"* (Boston: G. K. Hall, 1988), p. 57.

55. Cage, "Preface to 'Lecture on the Weather,'" in *Empty Words*, p. 3.

56. David S. Gross, "Deconstruction and the Denial of Meaning: On Sharon Cameron's *Writing Nature: Henry Thoreau's Journal*, A Review Essay," in *Genre*, vol. 21, no. 1 (Spring 1988), p. 97.

57. Philip F. Gura, "Language and Meaning: An American Tradition," in *American Literature*, vol. 53, no. 1 (March 1981), p. 10.

58. Note that Brown's remarks in his lecture "John Cage" (in Duckworth and Fleming, eds., *John Cage at Seventy-Five*) are critical rather than supportive. See John Cage with Daniel Charles, *For the Birds*, p. 113: "It is that aspect, the *impossibility of language*, that interests me at present." Brown's criticism concerns Cage's interest in the impossibility of language "instead of symbolism." Brown's original citation, quoting Carlyle, in Norman O. Brown, *Love's Body* (1966; reprint, Berkeley: University of California Press, 1990), p. 190, reads: "Broken speech; speech broken by silence. To let the silence in is symbolism. 'In symbol there is concealment, and yet revelation: here therefore, by Silence and by Speech acting together, comes a double significance.'" For Brown, symbolism is an essential unifier of brokenness. In his lecture "John Cage," "double significance" is then followed by "instead of words of silent power, the impossibility of language" (p. 110). "Words of silent power" is a citation from James Joyce, *Finnegans Wake* (1939; reprint, New York: Viking Press, 1959), p. 345. Brown is thus criticizing what he calls Cage's literalness—"Everything is taken literally, even the silence" (p. 110)—while professing his preference for the symbolism of Joyce's "words of silent power."

59. These paradoxes confounded Emerson as well. Gary Scharnhorst brought the following passage from Emerson's journal to my attention: "H.D.T. sends me a paper with the old fault of unlimited contradiction. The trick of his rhetoric is soon learned. It consists in substituting for the obvious word and thought its diametrical antagonist." Porte, ed., *Emerson in His Journals*, p. 313 (August–September 1843).

60. Porte, *Emerson and Thoreau*, p. 131.

61. Cage, Darmstadt Lecture, p. 2.

62. Among others, two studies consider those influences at greater length: for Cage, see David Wayne Patterson, "Appraising the Catchwords, c. 1942–1959: John Cage's Asian-Derived Rhetoric and the Historical Reference of Black Mountain College" (Ph.D. diss., Columbia University, 1996), pp. 58–179; for Thoreau, see Arthur Versluis, *American Transcendentalism and Asian Religions* (Oxford: Oxford University Press, 1993), especially pp. 79–99.

63. Cage, "List No. 2," in Richard Kostelanetz, ed., *John Cage*, pp. 138–139.

64. Christy, *The Orient in American Transcendentalism*, p. 190.

65. Tan, "'Taking a Nap,'" p. 41.

66. Christy, *The Orient in American Transcendentalism*, p. 23.

67. "After Antiquity: John Cage in Conversation with Peter Gena," in Gena and Brent, eds., *A John Cage Reader*, p. 178.

68. Cage, "Foreword," in *M* (unpaged).

69. Huang Po, *The Zen Teaching of Huang Po: On the Transmission of Mind*, John Blofeld, trans. (1958; reprint, New York: Grove Press, 1959), p. 58.

70. Versluis, *American Transcendentalism and Asian Religions*, p. 94. Versluis does, however, point out: "Now and then we find the most uncannily Taoist or Zen Buddhist observations in Thoreau's works: like them—though he could not have had any direct contact with those traditions—he wished to see truly, with the eye of an infant as it were" (p. 93).

71. Christy, *The Orient in American Transcendentalism*, p. 219.

72. Ibid., p. 230.

73. Ananda K. Coomaraswamy, *The Transformation of Nature in Art* (1934; reprint, New York: Dover Publications, 1956), pp. 37–38. Coomaraswamy's use of "imagist" is fortuitous, since in the next chapter I will place Cage in a context originating in a poetic movement called imagism.

THE TRANSPARENT EYE/I

1. Charles Olson, *Collected Prose*, Donald Allen and Benjamin Friedlander, eds. (Berkeley: University of California Press, 1997), p. 157.

2. Thoreau, *Journal*, p. 164 (probably October 1850).

3. William Carlos Williams, "Book Two: Sunday in the Park," in *Paterson* (1958; revised edition prepared by Christopher MacGowan, New York: New Directions, 1992), p. 46.

4. Nancy Willard, *Testimony of the Invisible Man: William Carlos Williams, Francis Ponge, Rainer Maria Rilke, Pablo Neruda* (Columbia: University of Missouri Press, 1970), p. 3.

5. Cage, "Introduction," in *I–VI*, p. 3.

6. Richard Fleming, "Introduction," in Fleming and Duckworth, eds., *John Cage at Seventy-Five*, p. 10.

7. Robert Creeley, "Introduction to Penguin *Selected Whitman*," in *The Collected Essays of Robert Creeley* (Berkeley: University of California Press, 1989), p. 10.

8. Cage, "Composition as Process," in *Silence*, p. 18.

9. Olson, "The View, Part Two: The Topological," in *The Special View of History*, p. 49.

10. Louis Zukofsky, "An Objective," in *Prepositions: The Collected Critical Essays of Louis Zukofsky, Expanded Edition* (1967; reprint, Berkeley: University of California Press, 1981), p. 15.

11. Gertrude Stein, "Composition as Explanation," in *Selected Writings of Gertrude Stein*, Carl Van Vechten, ed. (1946; reprint, New York: Random House, 1962), p. 513.

12. Cage, "Composition as Process," in *Silence*, p. 31.

13. William Barrett, *Irrational Man: A Study in Existential Philosophy* (1958; reprint, Garden City, N.Y.: Doubleday, 1962), p. 63. I have chosen Barrett's book as a source because, published in 1958, it expresses the philosophical underpinnings of an influential segment of the popular consciousness of the late 1950s and early 1960s, formative years for the writers to be discussed.

14. Ibid., p. 248.

15. Ibid., p. 249.

16. Ibid.

17. Ibid., p. 214.

18. William Carlos Williams, "Book One: The Delineaments of the Giants," in *Paterson*, p. 6.

19. Charles Olson, *Call Me Ishmael*, in *Collected Prose*, p. 17.

20. William Carlos Williams, *Selected Poems*, Charles Tomlinson, ed. (1976; reprint, New York: New Directions, 1985), p. xiii.

21. R. Buckminster Fuller, *Operating Manual for Spaceship Earth* (1969; reprint, New York: Pocket Books, 1970), p. 58.

22. Olson, "Human Universe," in *Collected Prose*, p. 162.

23. George Oppen, *The Collected Poems of George Oppen* (New York: New Directions, 1975), p. 190.

24. Williams, "Book One: The Delineaments of the Giants," in *Paterson*, p. 17.

25. Marjorie Perloff, *The Dance of the Intellect: Studies in the Poetry of the Pound Tradition* (Cambridge: Cambridge University Press, 1985), p. 22.

26. Albert Gelpi, *A Coherent Splendor: The American Poetic Renaissance 1910–1950* (Cambridge: Cambridge University Press, 1987), p. 184.

27. Waggoner, *American Poets from the Puritans to the Present*, p. 333. According to Waggoner, this definition was also mentioned by F. S. Flint in his "Imagisme" note in the March 1913 issue of *Poetry* magazine (p. 679).

28. Waggoner, *American Poets*, p. 341.

29. Ezra Pound, *Personae: The Collected Shorter Poems of Ezra Pound* (New York: New Directions, 1971), p. 109.

30. M. H. Abrams, preface to *The Mirror and the Lamp: Romantic Theory and the Critical Tradition* (1953; reprint, New York: Oxford University Press, 1977) (unpaged).

31. None of the poets to be discussed is either wholly objective or wholly projective. Consequently, during the course of this analysis the reader should assume that the division between projective and objective verse is directed toward predominant poetic tendencies rather than all-encompassing poetic traits.

32. "No other poet, unless it be Whitman, has been so important as Emerson to later poets, including the greatest of them." Waggoner, *American Poets*, p. 91.

33. "Craft Interview with Robert Creeley," in William Packard, ed., *The Craft of Poetry: Interviews from the "New York Quarterly"* (Garden City, N.Y.: Doubleday, 1974), p. 209. And according to Charles Olson there is a principle that, "when obeyed, is the reason why a projective poem can come into being. It is this: FORM IS NEVER MORE THAN AN EXTENSION OF CONTENT. (Or so it got phrased by one, R. Creeley, and it makes absolute sense to me, with this possible corollary, that right form, in any given poem, is the only and exclusively possible extension of content under hand.)" "Projective Verse," in Olson, *Collected Prose*, p. 240.

34. Olson, *Call Me Ishmael*, in *Collected Prose*, p. 18.

35. Emerson, "Discipline," from *Nature*, in *Selected Essays*, p. 57.

36. Emerson, "Introduction" to *Nature*, in ibid., p. 36.

37. Emerson, "Discipline," from *Nature*, in ibid., p. 58.

38. Olson, *Call Me Ishmael*, in *Collected Prose*, p. 17.

39. Paul Christensen, *Charles Olson: Call Him Ishmael* (Austin: University of Texas Press, 1979), p. 34.

40. Ibid., p. 36, p. 37.

41. Olson, *Call Me Ishmael*, in *Collected Prose*, p. 87.

42. Ibid., p. 19.

43. See John Taggart, "Call Me Isabel, Call Me Pierre: Charles Olson's Misreading of Melville," in *Boundary 2*, vol. 16, nos. 2–3 (1989), p. 261, where he asserts: "This identification of space in Melville as an exterior reality is a fundamental misreading. Not only does it praise Melville for what he isn't, a writer primarily concerned with depicting the external scene, but it also confuses a vital connection. This concerns the declaration of rivalry with the elements of external nature as the way to acquire the lost dimension of space *and* to disclose paternity. Such rivalry is Ahab's approach, and it results in disaster for himself and the crew."

44. Olson, *Call Me Ishmael,* in *Collected Prose,* p. 105.

45. Ibid., p. 86.

46. Olson, "A Bibliography on America for Ed Dorn," in *Collected Prose,* pp. 297–298.

47. Olson, "Projective Verse," in *Collected Prose,* p. 247.

48. Charles Olson, "The Kingfishers," in *The Collected Poems of Charles Olson,* George F. Butterick, ed. (Berkeley: University of California Press, 1987), p. 86.

49. George Butterick, "Charles Olson's 'The Kingfishers' and the Poetics of Change," in *American Poetry,* vol. 6, no. 2 (1989), p. 30.

50. Edward Dorn, "What I See in *The Maximus Poems,*" in *Views,* Donald Allen, ed. (San Francisco: Four Seasons Foundation, 1980), p. 29.

51. Ibid. Dorn continues, "Although sometimes it may be. But I doubt it."

52. Ibid., p. 37. Dorn goes on to say, "This same abstraction is the background for his intense ugliness too."

53. Ibid., p. 36.

54. Which can be regarded, along with symbolism and harmony, as characteristics of an active, controlling self. The connection between Emerson and Robert Duncan addresses this specifically. According to Stephen Fredman: "Like Emerson, Duncan works within a Platonic notion of harmony or correspondence. . . . But like Emerson and in distinction to Plato, Duncan believes that such harmony must be *actively* discovered by the poet through listening to language." Stephen Fredman, *The Grounding of American Poetry: Charles Olson and the Emersonian Tradition* (Cambridge: Cambridge University Press, 1993), p. 102 (emphasis added). Listening implies an objectivist approach; however, that harmony must be "actively discovered by the poet" through listening is a clear example of how the projectivist approach differs from objectivism.

55. Olson, "Projective Verse," in *Collected Prose,* p. 247.

56. Olson, "Human Universe," in *Collected Prose,* p. 158.

57. Michael Davidson, " 'To Eliminate the Draw': Narrative and Language in *Slinger,*" in Donald Wesling, ed., *Internal Resistances: The Poetry of Edward Dorn* (Berkeley: University of California Press, 1985), p. 131.

58. Edward Dorn, *Interviews,* Donald Allen, ed. (Bolinas, Calif.: Four Seasons Foundation, 1980), p. 27. This interview with Barry Alpert took place on July 31, 1972.

59. Ibid., p. 102. This interview with Stephen Fredman took place on March 7 and August 10, 1977.

60. Edward Dorn, *Gunslinger* (1975; reprint, Durham, N.C.: Duke University Press, 1989), p. xvii. The citation is from Marjorie Perloff's introduction.

61. Dorn, "Book III: The Winterbook" in ibid., p. 134.

62. Christensen, *Charles Olson*, p. 169. On the following page, Christensen also remarks that Robert Creeley and Robert Duncan "were closest to Olson, both in their admiration for him and in the extent to which they shared some of his ideas about writing. Personally, Olson was closer to Creeley perhaps than to any other man in his life."

63. Martin Duberman, *Black Mountain: An Exploration in Community* (1972; reprint, Gloucester, Mass.: Peter Smith, 1988), p. 347.

64. Olson, *Collected Poems*, p. 272. Note that the piece Olson is referring to, *Williams Mix* (Cage was composing it during the summer session at Black Mountain College, the same time—ca. July–August 1952—that Olson wrote his poem), was also criticized by Cage himself, and for the same reason. When asked about the piece (Kostelanetz, "Conversation with John Cage," in *John Cage*, p. 19), Cage replied: "Although my choices were controlled by chance operations, I was still making an object." The use of chance operations does not necessarily produce an indeterminate result. *Williams Mix* does indeed have a beginning and an end, thus existing within what Olson regarded as an out-of-date aesthetic. Where Olson and Cage disagree is on the question of intent. Although Cage attempts to remove himself from the process, Olson believed such attempts would be unfruitful. Once again, the position of self is the point of departure.

65. Ekbert Faas, ed., *Towards a New American Poetics: Essays and Interviews* (Santa Barbara: Black Sparrow Press, 1978), p. 176.

66. Robert Creeley, *Contexts of Poetry: Interviews, 1961–1971*, Donald Allen, ed. (Bolinas, Calif.: Four Seasons Foundation, 1973), p. 167. This interview with Lewis MacAdams took place in March 1967.

67. Kostelanetz, *Conversing with Cage*, p. 215 (1979).

68. Ron Silliman, *The New Sentence* (New York: Roof Books, 1987), p. 174.

69. Concerning Cage's "45' for a Speaker" (1954), William Fetterman writes: "The structure of having each line take a maximum of two seconds may be an application of Charles Olson's 'projective verse,' where one writes poetry according to the use of the breath in order to determine time lengths." Fetterman, *John Cage's Theatre Pieces: Notations and Performances* (Amsterdam: Harwood Academic Publishers, 1996), p. 206. Fetterman continues: "Cage knew Olson from Black Mountain College, but when asked if he was using Olson's idea, he replied that he did not really understand what Olson meant at the time, but that he liked the idea now." Olson's projective sense of breath differs from the method Cage uses in "45' for a Speaker": "Before writing this piece, I composed *34'46.776" for Two Pianists*. . . . Having been asked to speak at the Composers' Concourse in London (October 1954), I decided

to prepare for that occasion a lecture using the same structure, thus permitting the playing of music during the delivery of the speech. . . . When I applied the chance factor to the numerical rhythmic structure in the case of the speech, I obtained 39'16.95". However, when the text was completed, I found I was unable to perform it within that time-length. I needed more time. I made experiments, reading long lines as rapidly as I could. The result was two seconds for each line, 45' for the entire piece. Not all the text can be read comfortably even at this speed, but one can still try." John Cage, *Silence*, p. 146. When Olson remarks that "[v]erse now, 1950, if it is to go ahead, if it is to be of *essential* use, must, I take it, catch up and put into itself certain laws and possibilities of the breath, of the breathing of the man who writes as well as of his listenings" (Olson, "Projective Verse," in *Collected Prose*, p. 239), he certainly did not have in mind the kind of physical calisthenics Cage performed in order to make a reading of "45' for a Speaker" work within the chance-determined time frame he designed. However, that being said, Cage *does* become more concerned with breathing in his later work, to the point where it is even notated in his Charles Eliot Norton Lectures (see Cage, "Introduction," in *I–VI*, p. 5). Because he lived so long, it is important to keep track of time. Cage in 1988 (when Fetterman interviewed him) is not necessarily the Cage I address in this book. The Cage being considered here fits not with Olson but with the objectivists.

70. Kostelanetz, *Conversing with Cage*, p. 236 (1980).

71. Robert Creeley, *The Island* (1963), in *The Collected Prose of Robert Creeley* (1984; reprint, Berkeley: University of California Press, 1988), p. 101.

72. Robert Duncan, *The Opening of the Field* (1960; reprint, New York: New Directions, 1973), p. 11.

73. Duncan, "Often I Am Permitted to Return to a Meadow," in *The Opening of the Field*, p. 7.

74. Lee Bartlett, *The Sun Is But a Morning Star: Studies in West Coast Poetry and Poetics* (Albuquerque: University of New Mexico Press, 1989), p. 61.

75. Creeley, *The Island*, in *Collected Prose*, p. 173.

76. Emerson, "The American Scholar," in *Selected Essays*, pp. 86–87.

77. Emerson, "Language," from *Nature*, in ibid., p. 50.

78. Robert Duncan observes of Emerson's "Self-Reliance," "Today, in 1979, reading that essay, I find again how Emersonian my spirit is." Duncan, "The Self in Postmodern Poetry," in *Fictive Certainties: Essays by Robert Duncan* (New York: New Directions, 1985), p. 226. This appropriately brings the discussion of projective verse full circle: back to Emerson.

79. Christensen, *Charles Olson*, p. 77.

80. Herman Melville, "Chapter 11, Nightgown," in *Moby-Dick, or The White Whale* (New York: New American Library, 1980), p. 68.

81. Faas, ed., *Towards a New American Poetics*, p. 82.

82. Thoreau, *Journal*, p. 300 (November 10, 1851).

83. Peck, *Thoreau's Morning Work*, has already been cited as connecting Thoreau to the objectivists. Fredman's *Grounding of American Poetry* does so as well: "Thoreau demonstrates the necessary interdependence of two of the most salient, though seemingly contradictory, inclinations in American poetry: objectivism and transcendentalism" (p. 30). He then compares the work of Thoreau with that of Charles Olson, and he will later compare Emerson with Robert Duncan. Although my analysis also connects Duncan with Emerson (as well as with the other projectivists so far discussed), I do not compare Olson and Thoreau favorably; in fact, I see objectivism and transcendentalism as both contradictory of and independent from each other. In his preface, Fredman remarks: "This undertaking began in 1982 with the intuition that the projectivists and the transcendentalists share something in common" (p. ix). I agree, but I intend to prove through my analysis that the objectivists, Thoreau included, were neither transcendentalists nor projectivists.

84. George Oppen, "The Mind's Own Place," quoted in Michael Palmer, "On Objectivism," *Sulfur*, no. 26 (Spring 1990), p. 122.

85. Williams, "Book Two: Sunday in the Park," in *Paterson*, p. 84. The question of whether Williams was predominantly an objectivist poet is worth considering, since Williams's views changed in various periods of his life. This chapter excerpts quotations by Williams that establish an objectivist view. Could one just as likely collect quotations that emphasize his projectivist views? Perhaps; but in my opinion, much more material affirms an objective stance. As a result, I will treat Williams in the analysis that follows as an objectivist.

86. Williams, "Book One: The Delineaments of the Giants," in ibid., p. 17.

87. Oppen, "Three Poets," in *Poetry*, vol. 100, no. 5 (August 1962), p. 331, cited in Rachel Blau DuPlessis, "Objectivist Poetics and Political Vision: A Study of Oppen and Pound," in Burton Hatlen, ed., *George Oppen: Man and Poet* (Orono: University of Maine at Orono, National Poetry Foundation, 1981), p. 123.

88. Oppen, "Of Being Numerous," in *Collected Poems*, p. 167.

89. Oppen, "Route," in ibid., p. 195.

90. Melville, "Chapter 55: Of the Monstrous Pictures of Whales," in *Moby-Dick*, p. 262: "the great Leviathan is that one creature in the world which must remain unpainted to the last . . . there is no earthly way of finding out precisely what the whale really looks like."

91. Thoreau, *Journal*, p. 184 (February 14, 1851).

92. Barry Ahearn, *Zukofsky's "A": An Introduction* (Berkeley: University of California Press, 1983), p. 126.

93. William Carlos Williams, "A Beginning on the Short Story (Notes)," in *Selected Essays of William Carlos Williams* (1954; reprint, New York: New Directions, 1969), p. 303.

94. Ibid.

95. Cage, Darmstadt lecture, July 1990, p. 1.

96. Williams, "Beginning on the Short Story," in *Selected Essays*, p. 303.

97. Marjorie Perloff, *The Poetics of Indeterminacy: Rimbaud to Cage* (1981; reprint, Evanston, Ill.: Northwestern University Press, 1983), p. 106.

98. Willard, *Testimony of the Invisible Man*, p. 113.

99. "Craft Interview with Jackson MacLow," in Packard, ed., *The Craft of Poetry*, p. 250.

100. Williams, "Notes in Diary Form," in *Selected Essays*, p. 68. In contrast, Edward Dorn has said: "I've always been confused by those attempts to make language the same thing as the thing. I don't want to say again what Williams said ["No ideas but in things"]—in fact I don't want to say that at all." Dorn, *Interviews*, p. 47. This interview with Roy K. Okada took place on May 2, 1973.

101. Porte, *Emerson and Thoreau: Transcendentalists in Conflict*, p. 122.

102. Michael Heller, *Conviction's Net of Branches: Essays on the Objectivist Poets and Poetry* (Carbondale: Southern Illinois University Press, 1985), p. ix.

103. Zukofsky, "An Objective," in *Prepositions*, p. 12.

104. Heller, *Conviction's Net of Branches*, p. 23.

105. Charles Bernstein, *Content's Dream: Essays 1975–1984* (Los Angeles: Sun and Moon Press, 1986), p. 329.

106. Heller, *Conviction's Net of Branches*, p. 23.

107. Olson, "Human Universe," in *Collected Prose*, p. 157.

108. Williams, "Notes in Diary Form," in *Selected Essays*, p. 68.

109. Williams, "Book One: The Delineaments of the Giants," in *Paterson*, p. 18.

110. Ibid., p. 6.

111. Cage, "On Robert Rauschenberg, Artist, and His Work," in *Silence*, p. 108, cited in Marjorie Perloff, *The Poetics of Indeterminacy*, p. 313.

112. Oppen, "Of Being Numerous," in *Collected Poems*, p. 172.

113. David McAleavey, "Clarity and Process: Oppen's 'Of Being Numerous,'" in Hatlen, ed., *George Oppen*, p. 401.

114. "Craft Interview with Jackson MacLow," in Packard, ed., *The*

Craft of Poetry, p. 250: "Cage and, through his influence, I began composing by means of chance operations in the '50's in an attempt to escape the dominance of the ego—especially the personal passions—in art."

115. Perloff, *The Dance of the Intellect*, p. 35.

116. Stein, "Rooms," from *Tender Buttons*, in *Selected Writings*, p. 498.

117. Williams, "A 1 Pound Stein," in *Selected Essays*, p. 163.

118. Silliman, *The New Sentence*, p. 115.

119. Ahearn, *Zukofsky's "A"*, p. 203.

120. Bernstein, *Content's Dream*, p. 336.

121. Thoreau, *Journal*, p. 89 (September 14, 1841).

122. Kostelanetz, *Conversing with Cage*, p. 189 (1968).

123. Williams, "Book One: The Delineaments of the Giants" in *Paterson*, p. 30.

124. Oppen, "Of Being Numerous," in *Collected Poems*, p. 166.

125. Oppen, "Route," in ibid., p. 185.

126. Oppen, "Of Being Numerous," in ibid., p. 162.

127. Janice L. Doane, *Silence and Narrative: The Early Novels of Gertrude Stein* (Westport, Conn.: Greenwood Press, 1986), p. xi, quoting Stein, "Rooms," from *Tender Buttons*, in *Selected Writings*, p. 503.

128. Thoreau, *Journal*, p. 178 (January 4, 1851).

129. Doane, *Silence and Narrative*, p. xi.

130. Stein, "Rooms," from *Tender Buttons*, in *Selected Writings*, pp. 499–500.

131. Stein, "England," from *Geography and Plays* (1922; reprint, Madison: University of Wisconsin Press, 1993), p. 93, cited in Doane, *Silence and Narrative*, p. xii.

132. Stein, "What Happened," in *Geography and Plays*, p. 205, cited in Doane, *Silence and Narrative*, p. xii.

133. Doane, *Silence and Narrative*, p. xv (emphasis added).

134. Stein, "Rooms," from *Tender Buttons*, in *Selected Writings*, p. 501.

135. Williams, *The Collected Poems of William Carlos Williams, Volume I: 1909–1939*, A. Walton Litz and Christopher MacGowan, eds. (New York: New Directions, 1986), pp. 191–192.

136. Cage, "Lecture on Nothing," in *Silence*, p. 109.

137. Thoreau, *Journal*, p. 394 (April 29, 1852).

138. Ibid., p. 518 (January 21, 1853).

SILENCING THE SOUNDED SELF

1. Kostelanetz, *Conversing with Cage*, p. 218 (1975). Although Cage elsewhere again asserts that he wrote this speech when he was

twelve (Cage, *Empty Words*, p. 5), his biographer, David Revill (*The Roaring Silence: John Cage: A Life* [New York: Arcade Publishing, 1992], p. 30), and the critic Kostelanetz (*John Cage*, p. 45) claim that this text was written in 1927, when Cage was fifteen. (Further references to *Conversing with Cage*, abbreviated *CC*, and to *Empty Words*, abbreviated *EW*, will be included parenthetically in the text of this chapter.)

2. Cage, "Indeterminacy," in *Silence*, p. 261. (Further references to this work, abbreviated *S*, will be included parenthetically in the text of this chapter.)

3. At issue here is not whether Cage's assessment of Satie and Webern is accurate. His opinion, as presented in "Defense of Satie," is, in fact, debatable. Instead it is a question of whom Cage considered his predecessors.

4. Cage, "Defense of Satie," in Kostelanetz, *John Cage*, p. 81. I do not wish to imply, by contrast, that Ives *did* structure his pieces by means of harmony. Formally, Ives composed his music by duration as well. According to William Brooks, "Ives required himself to center his compositions in the domain of rhythm without relying on pitch to organize that domain" (William Brooks, "A Drummer-Boy Looks Back: Percussion in Ives's *Fourth Symphony*," in *Percussive Notes*, vol. 22, no. 6 [September 1984], p. 7). It is in the area of content, as a means of correspondent transcendence, that harmony plays such a central role in Ives's compositions.

5. Cage, "Defense of Satie," in Kostelanetz, *John Cage*, p. 81.

6. This is, of course, easier said than done. One could perhaps say that it requires at least one thought prior to the possibility of such listening: "I will listen without thought or preconception." However, having recognized the complexities involved, addressing this important issue further is beyond the scope of an analysis concerned more with compositional intention than with the realization of those intentions. One writer who has considered this issue in more detail is Daniel Herwitz, "John Cage," in *Making Theory/Constructing Art*, pp. 140–173.

7. Note that Cage uses "structure" to describe what might be traditionally called form, while using "form" to describe what would usually (especially in a literary sense) be called content.

8. Cage with Charles, *For the Birds*, p. 55.

9. Revill, *The Roaring Silence*, p. 85.

10. Calvin Tomkins, *The Bride and the Bachelors: Five Masters of the Avant-Garde* (1965; reprint, New York: Penguin Books, 1985), p. 97.

11. Cage, "Memoir," in Kostelanetz, *John Cage*, p. 77.

12. "[A]n important book for me was *The Perennial Philosophy* by Aldous Huxley, which is an anthology of remarks of people in different periods of history and from different cultures—that they are all saying the same thing, namely, a quiet mind is a mind that is free of its likes

and dislikes. You can become narrow-minded, literally, by only liking certain things, and disliking others. But you can become open-minded, literally, by giving up your likes and dislikes and becoming interested in things. I think Buddhists would say, 'As they are in and of themselves'" (*CC*, p. 231 [1984]). There is obviously a strong connection between this point of view and that of both Thoreau and objectivist poetry.

13. Aldous Huxley, *The Perennial Philosophy* (1945; reprint, New York: Harper and Row, 1970), p. 21.

14. Cage, "Memoir," in Kostelanetz, *John Cage*, p. 77.

15. It also connected musical and spiritual purposes that in 1948 Cage considered to be an important compositional concern: "I felt that an artist had an ethical responsibility to society to keep alive to the contemporary spiritual needs; I felt that if he did this, admittedly vague as it is a thing to do, his work would automatically carry with it a usefulness to others." Cage, "A Composer's Confessions," in Kostelanetz, ed., *John Cage: Writer*, p. 34.

16. "Translator's Introduction," in Huang Po, *The Zen Teaching of Huang Po*, p. 14.

17. Cage, "Tokyo Lecture and Three Mesostics," in Kostelanetz, ed., *John Cage: Writer*, p. 177: "The first time I saw the *I Ching* was in the San Francisco Public Library circa 1936. Lou Harrison introduced me to it. I did not use it at that time in any way other than to glance at it. Later in 1950 Christian Wolff gave me the Bollingen two-volume edition of the English translation by Cary F. Baynes of Richard Wilhelm's German translation with the introduction by C. G. Jung. This time I was struck immediately by the possibility of using the *I Ching* as a means for answering questions that had to do with numbers."

18. C. G. Jung, foreword to Richard Wilhelm, German trans., *The I Ching, or Book of Changes*, rendered into English by Cary F. Baynes (1950; reprint, 3d ed. (1967), Princeton: Princeton University Press, 1990), p. xxii.

19. Cage, "A Composer's Confessions," in *John Cage: Writer*, p. 43. As for the second piece: "[T]o compose and have performed a composition using as instruments nothing but twelve radios. It will be my *Imaginary Landscape No. 4.*"

20. Cage, "Happy New Ears!" in *A Year from Monday*, p. 31.

21. Cage with Charles, *For the Birds*, p. 80.

22. Kostelanetz, "John Cage: Some Random Remarks," in *John Cage*, pp. 195–196. And this became, for Cage, the purpose of *4'33"* as well: "I don't sit down to do it; I turn my attention toward it. I realize that it's going on continuously. So, more and more, my attention, as now, is on it" (Duckworth, "Anything I Say Will Be Misunderstood: An Interview with John Cage," in Fleming and Duckworth, eds., *John Cage at Seventy-Five*, p. 22).

23. John Cage, *Variations III* (New York: Henmar Press, 1963).

24. Kostelanetz, "Conversation with John Cage," in *John Cage*, p. 19.

25. Cage, *Variations III* (page 4 of list), from the John Cage papers, Wesleyan University Archives.

26. Kostelanetz, "John Cage: Some Random Remarks," in *John Cage*, p. 197.

27. Cage's definition of what constitutes poetry is reductive at best. It does, however, help to place several of his writings (which would include those so far discussed, "Lecture on Nothing" and "Lecture on Something") in the context of poetry. It is not my purpose here to define poetry; I would, however, submit that poetry is usually created by writers who consider it to be poetry. This being the case, I regard the lectures I have mentioned as Cage regarded them: as poetry.

28. For reasons that will become apparent as the analysis progresses, this book ends in 1974 with the completion of "Empty Words." Cage's mesostics are brilliantly conceived poetry. However, my concern lies with the connection between music and text; the mesostic form becomes important for both after the completion of "Empty Words," when Cage begins his mesostic series on James Joyce's *Finnegans Wake*.

29. Cage, "Diary: Audience 1966," in *A Year from Monday*, p. 50.

30. Cage, "Diary: Emma Lake Music Workshop 1965," in *A Year from Monday*, p. 21.

31. Cage, "Diary: How to Improve the World (You Will Only Make Matters Worse) 1965," in *A Year from Monday*, p. 3.

32. According to the Map and Geographic Information Center at the University of New Mexico, the distance between Rochester and Philadelphia is 336 miles. Using the method recommended by the American Automobile Association, I simply divided this distance by 50 miles per hour.

33. Cage's hexagram notation uses what look like V's for the broken lines; he puts a circle through a changing straight line and around the *V* for a changing broken line.

34. The other hexagrams translate, from left to right: 3. 58; 4. 29 changing to 18 (part II); 5. 46 changing to 24 (this incorrectly notated as 23 at the top but corrected when placed in the roman numeral structure); 6. 10; 7. 28 changing to 43 (which is placed in part IV since the 28 puts the total of part III over 100); 8. 50; 9. 55 (part IV); 10. 40 changing to 33; 11. 17 changing to 61 (part V); 12. 52 changing to 43; 13. 51 changing to 36 (which is not used in part VI, since 51 puts the total past 100).

35. Sometimes the last number makes it go over. For example, 63, 5, and 30 equal 98, thus requiring one more chance operation; this turns up as 21, totaling 119.

36. Revill, *The Roaring Silence*, p. 215.

37. Order of published text: I. 63, 5, 30, 21; II. 58, 29, 18; III. 46, 24, 10, 28; IV. 43, 50, 55; V. 40, 33, 17, 61; VI. 52, 43, 51. Order of texts as written in notebook: 51, 50, 43, 33, 46, 21, 61, 43, 61 (this is actually 63), 52, 55, 46, 58, 18, 29, 40, 28, 43, 30, 24, 17, 10, 5.

38. An abbreviation for "could" that Cage used often.

39. Cage, "Diary: Audience 1966," in *A Year from Monday*, p. 50. The references are to Marshall McLuhan, James Joyce, and Norman O. Brown.

40. Cage, *Silence*, p. x. "As I see it, poetry is not prose simply because poetry is in one way or another formalized."

41. Cage with Charles, *For the Birds*, p. 151.

42. I am not as sure about Duchamp as Cage was. I find that while Cage, like Thoreau, looks outward to the world, Duchamp's work is far more concerned with the inward direction of human intellect.

43. Cage with Charles, *For the Birds*, pp. 233–234.

44. Matthiessen, *American Renaissance*, p. 30, p. 44.

45. Cage with Charles, *For the Birds*, p. 113. Cage includes a footnote: "I have since made *Music of Thoreau* from it; it's the work I entitled *Mureau*, which I myself performed in concert."

46. Cage, *M*, first page of "Foreword" (unpaged).

47. Ibid., (second page of "Foreword").

48. Cage, "Mureau," in ibid., p. 35. Line endings and typefaces printed here vary somewhat from the original.

49. Revill, *The Roaring Silence*, p. 249. Cage himself mentions the date he spoke with McNaughton in his introduction to "Empty Words" (Cage, *Empty Words*, p. 11).

50. Cage's deduction need not be seen as a rationalization, since such thinking was in the air among Germans of Schoenberg's era. Martin Heidegger, for example, remarks in "The Origin of the Work of Art" (1935–1936) that "[e]ach answer remains in force as an answer only as long as it is rooted in questioning." Heidegger, *Poetry, Language, Thought*, Albert Hofstadter, trans. (New York: Harper and Row, 1971), p. 71.

51. William Brooks, in an analysis of *Songbooks* (1970), writes convincingly of a corresponding inclusion of choice in Cage's music. Brooks, "Choice and Change in Cage's Recent Music," in Gena and Brent, eds., *A John Cage Reader*, pp. 82–100. However, whereas Brooks maintains "that which is arrived at by choice is in no sense preferable to that arrived at by chance" (p. 97), my analysis will show that intention, while coexisting with non-intention, was *required* in order to achieve nondualism in "Empty Words."

52. Cage goes on to describe the complete process: "In the second one, the phrases are gone, and in the third part the words are gone, ex-

cept those that have only one syllable. And in the last one, everything is gone but letters and silences."

53. The connection to ideograms likely points both to Cage's familiarity with Pound and to Chinese-language orthography.

54. Ezra Pound, *ABC of Reading* (1934; reprint, New York: New Directions, 1960), p. 21.

55. This, together with the inclusion of Thoreau's drawings (which, as Cage mentioned in the introduction to part two, are specifically placed in the text through chance operations), refutes Marjorie Perloff's contention that "[t]he 'score' of "Empty Words," recently published, is, like the earlier one of "Mureau," fairly uninteresting, for everything here depends on Cage's enormous register, his astonishing timbre, his individual timing and articulation. Such dependence on *opsis* . . . is, of course, a limitation; we have to attend the performance in order to respond to Cage's language construct." Perloff, *The Poetics of Indeterminacy*, pp. 337–338. Cage's elaborate instructions, are, I would argue, directions for reading and the text a score for performance. I find the published versions of both "Mureau" and "Empty Words" immensely interesting. Granted, Cage's performances of his texts were extraordinary; however, this does not imply that his presence is a necessary part of experiencing his poetry.

56. "Mike Wallace Asks John Cage: How's That Again?" *New York Post*, June 10, 1958, p. 47.

57. Gagne and Caras, *Soundpieces*, pp. 78–79.

58. Perloff, *The Poetics of Indeterminacy*, pp. 315–316.

59. Duncan, "Towards an Open Universe," in *Fictive Certainties*, p. 82.

60. Charles Olson, *Causal Mythology* (San Francisco: Four Seasons Foundation, 1969), p. 2.

61. Thoreau, "Conclusion," in *"Walden" and Other Writings*, p. 297.

62. This concern can be found as early as the late 1950s: "At Darmstadt I was talking about the reason back of pulverization and fragmentation: for instance, using syllables instead of words in a vocal text, letters instead of syllables." From his lecture "Indeterminacy: New Aspect of Form in Instrumental and Electronic Music" (1958) published, in part, as "How to Pass, Kick, Fall, and Run" in Cage, *A Year from Monday*, p. 136.

WORKS CITED

Abrams, M. H. *The Mirror and the Lamp: Romantic Theory and the Critical Tradition.* 1953; reprint, New York: Oxford University Press, 1977.

Ahearn, Barry. *Zukofsky's "A": An Introduction.* Berkeley and Los Angeles: University of California Press, 1983.

Barrett, William. *Irrational Man: A Study in Existential Philosophy.* 1958; reprint, Garden City, N.Y.: Doubleday, 1962.

Bartlett, Lee. *The Sun Is But a Morning Star: Studies in West Coast*

Poetry and Poetics. Albuquerque: University of New Mexico Press, 1989.

Bernstein, Charles. *Content's Dream: Essays 1975–1984.* Los Angeles: Sun and Moon Press, 1986.

Block, Geoffrey, and J. Peter Burkholder, eds. *Charles Ives and the Classical Tradition.* New Haven: Yale University Press, 1996.

Brooks, William. "A Drummer-Boy Looks Back: Percussion in Ives's *Fourth Symphony.*" *Percussive Notes,* vol. 22, no. 6 (September 1984): 4–45.

Brown, Norman O. *Love's Body.* 1966; reprint, Berkeley and Los Angeles, Calif.: University of California Press, 1990.

Burbick, Joan. *Thoreau's Alternative History: Changing Perspectives on Nature, Culture, and Language.* Philadelphia: University of Pennsylvania Press, 1987.

Burkholder, J. Peter. *All Made of Tunes: Charles Ives and the Uses of Musical Borrowing.* New Haven: Yale University Press, 1995.

———. *Charles Ives: The Ideas Behind the Music.* New Haven: Yale University Press, 1985.

———, ed. *Charles Ives and His World.* Princeton: Princeton University Press, 1996.

Butterick, George. "Charles Olson's 'The Kingfishers' and the Poetics of Change." *American Poetry,* vol. 6, no. 2 (1989): 28–59.

Cage, John. *I–VI (The Charles Eliot Norton Lectures 1988- 1989).* Cambridge: Harvard University Press, 1990.

———. "Darmstadt Lecture." Unpublished lecture given at the Ferienkurse für Neue Musik, Darmstadt, Germany, July 1990.

———. "Diary: Audience 1966" (manuscript pages). John Cage papers, Wesleyan University Archives.

———. *Empty Words: Writings '73–'78.* Middletown, Conn.: Wesleyan University Press, 1979.

———. *M: Writings '67–'72.* Middletown, Conn.: Wesleyan University Press, 1973.

———. *Silence: Lectures and Writings.* Middletown, Conn.: Wesleyan University Press, 1961.

———. *Themes and Variations.* Barrytown, N.Y.: Station Hill Press, 1982.

———. *Variations III.* New York: Henmar Press, 1963.

———. "Variations III" (page 4 of list). John Cage papers, Wesleyan University Archives.

———. *A Year from Monday: New Lectures and Writings.* Middletown, Conn.: Wesleyan University Press, 1967.

Cage, John, with Daniel Charles. *For the Birds.* London: Marion Boyars, 1981.

Cameron, Sharon. *Writing Nature: Henry Thoreau's "Journal."* 1985; reprint, Chicago: University of Chicago Press, 1989.

Carlyle, Thomas. *On Heroes, Hero Worship and the Heroic in History.* Carl Niemeyer, ed. Lincoln: University of Nebraska Press, 1966.

Cavell, Stanley. *The Senses of Walden: An Expanded Edition.* 1972; reprint, Chicago: University of Chicago Press, 1981.

Chase, Gilbert. *America's Music: From the Pilgrims to the Present.* 1955; rev. 3d ed., Urbana: University of Illinois Press, 1987.

Ch'maj, Betty E. "The Journey and the Mirror: Emerson and the American Arts." *Prospects,* vol. 10 (1985): 353–408.

Christensen, Paul. *Charles Olson: Call Him Ishmael.* Austin: University of Texas Press, 1979.

Christy, Arthur. *The Orient in American Trancendentalism: A Study of Emerson, Thoreau, and Alcott.* New York: Columbia University Press, 1932.

Collins, Christopher. *The Uses of Observation: A Study of Correspondential Vision in the Writings of Emerson, Thoreau, and Whitman.* The Hague: Mouton, 1971.

Coomaraswamy, Ananda K. *The Transformation of Nature in Art.* 1934; reprint, New York: Dover Publications, 1956.

Cowell, Henry, ed. *American Composers on American Music.* 1933; reprint, New York: Frederick Ungar, 1962.

Cowell, Henry, and Sidney Cowell. *Charles Ives and His Music.* 1955; reprint, New York: Da Capo Press, 1983.

Creeley, Robert. *The Collected Essays of Robert Creeley.* Berkeley and Los Angeles: University of California Press, 1989.

———. *The Collected Prose of Robert Creeley.* 1984; reprint, Berkeley and Los Angeles: University of California Press, 1988.

———. *Contexts of Poetry: Interviews, 1961–1971.* Donald Allen, ed. Bolinas, Calif.: Four Seasons Foundation, 1973.

DeLio, Thomas. *Circumscribing the Open Universe.* New York: University Press of America, 1984.

Doane, Janice L. *Silence and Narrative: The Early Novels of Gertrude Stein.* Westport, Conn.: Greenwood Press, 1986.

Dorn, Edward. *Gunslinger.* 1975; reprint, Durham, N.C.: Duke University Press, 1989.

———. *Interviews.* Donald Allen, ed. Bolinas, Calif.: Four Seasons Foundation, 1980.

———. *Views.* Donald Allen, ed. San Francisco: Four Seasons Foundation, 1980.

Duberman, Martin. *Black Mountain: An Exploration in Community.* 1972; reprint, Gloucester, Mass.: Peter Smith, 1988.

Duncan, Robert. *Fictive Certainties: Essays by Robert Duncan.* New York: New Directions, 1985.

———. *The Opening of the Field.* 1960; reprint, New York: New Directions, 1973.

Ellison, Julie. *Emerson's Romantic Style.* Princeton: Princeton University Press, 1984.

Emerson, Edward Waldo. *Henry Thoreau: As Remembered by a Young Friend.* Boston: Houghton Mifflin, 1917.

Emerson, Ralph Waldo. *Emerson's Essays* (First and Second Series). 1926; reprint, New York: Harper and Row, 1951.

———. *Selected Essays.* Larzer Ziff, ed. New York: Penguin Books, 1982.

Faas, Ekbert, ed. *Towards a New American Poetics: Essays and Interviews.* Santa Barbara: Black Sparrow Press, 1978.

Feder, Stuart. *Charles Ives: "My Father's Song": A Psychoanalytic Biography.* New Haven: Yale University Press, 1992.

Fetterman, William. *John Cage's Theatre Pieces: Notations and Performances.* Amsterdam: Harwood Academic Publishers, 1996.

Fleming, Richard, and William Duckworth, eds. *John Cage at Seventy-Five.* Lewisburg, Pa.: Bucknell University Press, 1989.

Fredman, Stephen. *The Grounding of American Poetry: Charles Olson and the Emersonian Tradition.* Cambridge: Cambridge University Press, 1993.

Fuller, R. Buckminster. *Operating Manual for Spaceship Earth.* 1969; reprint, New York: Pocket Books, 1970.

Gagne, Cole, and Tracy Caras. *Soundpieces: Interviews with American Composers.* London: Scarecrow Press, 1982.

Gelpi, Albert. *A Coherent Splendor: The American Poetic Renaissance, 1910–1950.* Cambridge: Cambridge University Press, 1987.

Gena, Peter, and Jonathan Brent, eds. *A John Cage Reader in Celebration of His 70th Birthday.* New York: C. F. Peters, 1982.

Goodman, Russell B. *American Philosophy and the Romantic Tradition.* Cambridge: Cambridge University Press, 1990.

Gross, David S. "Deconstruction and the Denial of Meaning: On Sharon Cameron's *Writing Nature: Henry Thoreau's Journal,* A Review Essay." *Genre,* vol. 21, no. 1 (Spring 1988): 93–106.

Gura, Philip F. "Language and Meaning: An American Tradition." *American Literature,* vol. 53, no. 1 (March 1981): 1–21.

Harding, Walter. *The Variorum "Walden."* 1962; reprint, New York: Washington Square Press, 1963.

Harding, Walter, and Michael Meyer. *The New Thoreau Handbook.* New York: New York University Press, 1980.

Hatlen, Burton, ed. *George Oppen: Man and Poet.* Orono: National Poetry Foundation, University of Maine at Orono, 1981.

Heidegger, Martin. *Poetry, Language, Thought.* Albert Hofstadter, trans. New York: Harper and Row, 1971.

Heller, Michael. *Conviction's Net of Branches: Essays on the Objectivist Poets and Poetry.* Carbondale: Southern Illinois University Press, 1985.

Hertz, David Michael. *Angels of Reality: Emersonian Unfoldings in Wright, Stevens, and Ives.* Carbondale: Southern Illinois University Press, 1993.

Herwitz, Daniel. *Making Theory/Constructing Art: On the Authority of the Avant-Garde.* Chicago: University of Chicago Press, 1993.

Hitchcock, H. Wiley. *Ives: A Survey of the Music.* 1977; reprint, Brooklyn: Institute for Studies in American Music, 1985.

Huang Po. *The Zen Teaching of Huang Po: On the Transmission of Mind.* John Blofeld, trans. 1958; reprint, New York: Grove Press, 1959.

Huxley, Aldous. *The Perennial Philosophy.* 1945; reprint, New York: Harper and Row, 1970.

Ives, Charles E. *Central Park in the Dark.* Jacques-Louis Monod, ed., with notes by John Kirkpatrick. Hillsdale, N.Y.: Boelke-Bomart, 1973.

———. *"Essays before a Sonata," "The Majority," and Other Writings.* Howard Boatwright, ed. New York: W. W. Norton, 1970.

———. *Memos.* John Kirkpatrick, ed. 1972; reprint, New York: W. W. Norton, 1991.

———. *Second Pianoforte Sonata, "Concord, Mass., 1840–1860,"* 2d ed. New York: Arrow Music Press, 1947.

Johns, Jasper. "Sketchbook Notes." In Richard Francis, *Jasper Johns.* New York: Abbeville Press, 1984.

Joyce, James. *Finnegans Wake.* 1939; reprint, New York: Viking Press, 1959.

Kant, Immanuel. *Prolegomena to Any Future Metaphysics.* Carus translation revised by Lewis White Beck. Indianapolis: Bobbs-Merrill/ Library of Liberal Arts, 1950.

Kostelanetz, Richard. *Conversing with Cage.* New York: Limelight Editions, 1988.

———, ed. *John Cage.* 1970; reprint, New York: Da Capo Press, 1991.

———, ed. *John Cage: Writer: Previously Uncollected Pieces.* New York: Limelight Editions, 1993.

Leonard, George J. *Into the Light of Things: The Art of the Commonplace from Wordsworth to John Cage.* Chicago: University of Chicago Press, 1994.

Lopez, Michael. "De-Transcendentalizing Emerson." *ESQ: A Journal of the American Renaissance,* vol. 34, 1st and 2d quarters (1988): 77–139.

Matthiessen, F. O. *American Renaissance: Art and Expression in the Age of Emerson and Whitman.* New York: Oxford University Press, 1941.

Mellers, Wilfred. *Music in a New Found Land: Themes and Developments in the History of American Music.* New York: Alfred A. Knopf, 1965.

Melville, Herman. *Moby-Dick, or The White Whale.* New York: New American Library, 1980.

Myerson, Joel, ed. *Critical Essays on Henry David Thoreau's "Walden."* Boston: G. K. Hall, 1988.

Nicholls, David. *American Experimental Music, 1890–1940.* Cambridge: Cambridge University Press, 1990.

———. "The Great American Borrower." *Times Literary Supplement* (October 18, 1996): 18–19.

Olson, Charles. *Causal Mythology.* San Francisco: Four Seasons Foundation, 1969.

———. *The Collected Poems of Charles Olson.* George F. Butterick, ed. Berkeley and Los Angeles: University of California Press, 1987.

———. *Collected Prose.* Donald Allen and Benjamin Friedlander, eds. Berkeley and Los Angeles: University of California Press, 1997.

———. *The Special View of History.* Ann Charters, ed. Berkeley, Calif.: Oyez, 1970.

Oppen, George. *The Collected Poems of George Oppen.* New York: New Directions, 1975.

Owen, Stephen. *Traditional Chinese Poetry and Poetics: Omen of the World.* Madison: University of Wisconsin Press, 1985.

Packard, William, ed. *The Craft of Poetry: Interviews from the "New York Quarterly."* Garden City, N.Y.: Doubleday, 1974.

Palmer, Michael. "On Objectivism." *Sulfur,* no. 26 (Spring 1990): 117–126.

Patterson, David Wayne. "Appraising the Catchwords, c. 1942–1959: John Cage's Asian-Derived Rhetoric and the Historical Reference of Black Mountain College." Ph.D. diss., Columbia University, 1996.

Paul, Sherman. "The Wise Silence: Sound as the Agency of Correspondence in Thoreau." *New England Quarterly,* vol. 22, no. 4 (December 1949): 511–527.

Pearce, Roy Harvey. *The Continuity of American Poetry.* 1961; reprint, 2d ed., Middletown, Conn.: Wesleyan University Press, 1987.

Peck, H. Daniel. *Thoreau's Morning Work: Memory and Perception in "A Week on the Concord and Merrimack Rivers," the Journal, and "Walden."* New Haven: Yale University Press, 1990.

Perlis, Vivian. *Charles Ives Remembered: An Oral History*. New Haven: Yale University Press, 1974.

Perloff, Marjorie. The *Dance of the Intellect: Studies in the Poetry of the Pound Tradition*. Cambridge: Cambridge University Press, 1985.

———. *The Poetics of Indeterminacy: Rimbaud to Cage*. 1981; reprint, Evanston, Ill.: Northwestern University Press, 1983.

Perloff, Marjorie, and Charles Junkerman, eds. *John Cage: Composed in America*. Chicago: University of Chicago Press, 1994.

Perry, Rosalie Sandra. *Charles Ives and the American Mind*. Kent, Ohio: Kent State University Press, 1974.

Porte, Joel. *Emerson and Thoreau: Transcendentalists in Conflict*. Middletown, Conn.: Wesleyan University Press, 1966.

———. *In Respect to Egotism: Studies in American Romantic Writing*. Cambridge: Cambridge University Press, 1991.

———, ed. *Emerson in His Journals*. Cambridge: Belknap Press of Harvard University Press, 1982.

Pound, Ezra. *ABC of Reading*. 1934; reprint, New York: New Directions, 1960.

———. *Personae: The Collected Shorter Poems of Ezra Pound*. New York: New Directions, 1971.

Pritchett, James W. "The Development of Chance Techniques in the Music of John Cage, 1950–1956." Ph.D. diss., New York University, 1988.

———. *The Music of John Cage*. Cambridge: Cambridge University Press, 1993.

Rees, William, ed. *French Poetry: 1820–1950*. New York: Penguin Books, 1990.

Revill, David. *The Roaring Silence: John Cage: A Life*. New York: Arcade Publishing, 1992.

Rhoads, Kenneth W. "Thoreau: The Ear and the Music." *American Literature*, vol. 46, no. 3 (November 1974): 313–328.

Rossiter, Frank R. *Charles Ives and His America*. New York: Liveright, 1975.

Silliman, Ron. *The New Sentence*. New York: Roof Books, 1987.

Starr, Larry. *A Union of Diversities: Style in the Music of Charles Ives*. New York: Schirmer Books, 1992.

Steele, Jeffrey. *The Representation of the Self in the American Renaissance*. Chapel Hill: University of North Carolina Press, 1987.

Stein, Gertrude. *Geography and Plays*. 1922; reprint, Madison: University of Wisconsin Press, 1993.

———. *Selected Writings of Gertrude Stein*, Carl Van Vechten, ed. 1946; reprint, New York: Random House, 1962.

Taggart, John. "Call Me Isabel, Call Me Pierre: Charles Olson's Misreading of Melville." *Boundary 2*, vol. 16, nos. 2–3 (1989): 255–275.

Thoreau, Henry David. *Journal*. Bradford Torrey and Francis H. Allen, eds. 1906; reprint, New York: Dover Publications, 1962.

———. *"Walden" and Other Writings*, Brooks Atkinson, ed. New York: Modern Library, 1937.

Tomkins, Calvin. *The Bride and the Bachelors: Five Masters of the Avant-Garde*. 1965; reprint, New York: Penguin Books, 1985.

Van Doren, Mark. *Henry David Thoreau: A Critical Study*. 1916; reprint, New York: Russell and Russell, 1961.

———, ed. *The Portable Walt Whitman*. 1945; reprint, New York: The Viking Press, 1973.

Versluis, Arthur. *American Transcendentalism and Asian Religions*. Oxford: Oxford University Press, 1993.

Waggoner, Hyatt H. *American Poets from the Puritans to the Present*. 1968; rev. ed., Baton Rouge: Louisiana State University Press, 1984.

Wallace, Mike. "Mike Wallace Asks John Cage: How's That Again?" *New York Post* (June 10, 1958): 47.

Walls, Laura Dassow. *Seeing New Worlds: Henry David Thoreau and Nineteenth-Century Natural Science*. Madison: University of Wisconsin Press, 1995.

Wesling, Donald, ed. *Internal Resistances: The Poetry of Edward Dorn*. Berkeley and Los Angeles: University of California Press, 1985.

Wilhelm, Richard. *The I Ching or Book of Changes*. German trans., rendered into English by Cary F. Baynes. 1950; reprint, 3d ed. (1967), Princeton: Princeton University Press, 1990.

Willard, Nancy. *Testimony of the Invisible Man: William Carlos Williams, Francis Ponge, Rainer Maria Rilke, Pablo Neruda*. Columbia: University of Missouri Press, 1970.

Williams, William Carlos. *The Collected Poems of William Carlos Williams, Volume I: 1909–1939*. A. Walton Litz and Christopher MacGowan, eds. New York: New Directions, 1986.

———. *Paterson*. 1958; revised edition prepared by Christopher MacGowan, New York: New Directions, 1992.

———. *Selected Essays of William Carlos Williams*. 1954; reprint, New York: New Directions, 1969.

———. *Selected Poems*. Charles Tomlinson, ed. 1976; reprint, New York, New Directions, 1985.

Wright, David, ed. *The Penguin Book of English Romantic Verse*. 1968; reprint, Baltimore: Penguin Books, 1970.

Yates, Peter. *Twentieth-Century Music: Its Evolution from the End of the Harmonic Era into the Present Era of Sound*. New York: Pantheon Books, 1967.

Zukofsky, Louis. *"A."* Berkeley and Los Angeles: University of California Press, 1978.

———. *Prepositions: The Collected Critical Essays of Louis Zukofsky, Expanded Edition.* 1967; reprint, Berkeley and Los Angeles: University of California Press, 1981.

INDEX

Abrams, M. H., 67, 74, 77
acceptance, and coexistence, 35–36
adhesiveness, xxii
Ahearn, Barry, 77, 80
All the Way Around and Back (Ives), 21
ambient circumstances, 98–99
artistic coexistence. *See* coexistence

artistic control. *See* control
Asian philosophy, 56–57, 91–92.
  See also Zen Buddhism

Barrett, William, 63–64, 147n13
Bartlett, Lee, 74
Basho, xxi, xxii
Beethoven, Ludwig van
  Cage's views on, 86–87, 136n20
  Ives's views on, 16–17

extramusical references
in Cage's aesthetic, 32–33
in Ives Concord Sonata, 22–23
in Ives's works, 21, 24

Feder, Stuart, 128n4, 132n7,
137n48, 138n58
Fetterman, William, 150–151n69
First Construction in Metal
(Cage), 89
form, Cage's use of term, 155n7
"45' for a Speaker" (Cage), 150–
151n69
4'33" (Cage), xxii, 52–53, 94–95,
96, 129n13, 144n46, 156n22
Fourth of July (Ives), 23, 137–
138n48
Fredman, Stephen, 152n83
Fuller, Buckminster, 65
future, in Thoreau's aesthetic, 36

Gelpi, Albert, 66, 67
Goodman, Russell, 10
Gross, David S., 54–55
Gunslinger (Dorn), 71–72
Gura, Philip F., 55

Harding, Walter, 35, 43
harmony
in Cage's and Ives's aesthetics,
136n20
Cage's views on, 86–87
and Ives, 17, 155n4
and nature, 87–88
perception of, 88
Harrison, Lou, 92, 156n17
Heidegger, Martin, 64, 158n50
Heisenberg, Werner, 65
Heller, Michael, 78
hero, concept of, 35
Hertz, David Michael, 137n48
Herwitz, Daniel, 129n13

"History" (Emerson), 10
Hitchcock, H. Wiley, 21, 23, 26,
27, 132n7
Holidays Symphony (Ives), 24
Homer, Iliad, 35
Huang Po, 56, 57
humanity, and nature, 12–14, 64–
65, 76
in Cage's aesthetic, 33
in Emerson's aesthetic, 19–20,
33–34
in Olson's aesthetic, 68–71
in Thoreau's aesthetic, 34
in Thoreau's and Cage's aesthetics, 29
Huxley, Aldous, 155–156n12
The Perennial Philosophy, 91

I Ching, 93–94, 103–104, 107,
156n17
idealism
in Cage's aesthetic, 32–33
in Emerson's aesthetic, 10, 11–
14, 19, 134n6
in Ives's aesthetic, 15–16
in Thoreau's aesthetic, 29–30,
43
Iliad (Homer), 35
Imaginary Landscape No. 4
(Cage), 156n19
imagism, 66, 141n12, 146n73
"In a Station of the Metro"
(Pound), 66
"In the Night" (Ives), 25
indeterminacy, 65, 95–98
intellect, in Emerson's aesthetic,
12, 19–20
intention. See also non-intention
and Cage, 129n13
and Cage "Empty Words,"
158n51
vs. non-intention, xx, xxii

Tomlinson, Charles, 65
"A Toss, for John Cage" (Olson), 72
transcendental correspondence, 7, 9, 20–21, 28, 129n13. *See also* transcendentalism
and Ives, 26–28
transcendentalism, 5–7, 131–132n6. *See also* transcendental correspondence
and Ives, 26
and objectivism, 152n83
transparencies, use of in Cage works, 96–98

unity, 9–28
in Emerson's aesthetic, 11–14, 18–19, 133n12
in Ives's aesthetic, 15, 16, 17
and the "Oversoul," 21
and Thoreau, 56
of words and things, 116, 122

Variations (Cage), 95–96
Variations III (Cage), 96–97, 98–100
Versluis, Arthur, 57, 146n70

Waggoner, Hyatt H., 4, 66, 68
Walden (Thoreau), 34–46, 125, 139–140n5, 139n2, 139n3
compared with *Journal*, 48
and symbolism, 54–55
Walden Pond, 30–31
Wallace, Mike, 122–123
Washington's Birthday (Ives), 21

Webern, Anton, 86–87, 136n20
Wesleyan University Archives, 101, 107
Whitman, Walt, 29, 63
Willard, Nancy, 62, 78
Williams, William Carlos, xvi, 141n12
and Heidegger, 64–65
on nature, 77
objective verse of, xix
and objectivism, 65, 152n85
Paterson, 75–76
on poetry, 78
and the self, 79
and silence, 81
and Thoreau's aesthetic, 62
"To Have Done Nothing," 82–83
Williams Mix (Cage), 98, 150n64
Wolff, Christian, 156n17
Wordsworth, William, 129n13

Yates, Peter, 130–131n1
A Year from Monday (Cage), 100, 106

Zen Buddhism. *See also* Asian philosophy
and Cage, 45, 57
and chance operations, 93–94
and non-intention, xx
and silence, 92
and Thoreau, 146n70
The Zen Teaching of Huang Po, 92
Zukofsky, Louis, xix, 63, 77, 78–79, 80